I0673230

Story Sprouts

CBW-LA Writing Day I Exercises and Anthology
2013

Story Sprouts: CBW-LA Writing Day Exercises and Anthology 2013
Anthology Copyright © 2013 by CBW-LA Publications

Individual contributions © the Authors

All rights reserved. No part of this publication may be reproduced,
distributed, or transmitted in any form or by any means, including
photocopying, recording, or other electronic or mechanical methods,
without the prior written permission of the publisher, except in the case
of brief quotations embodied in critical reviews and certain other
noncommercial uses permitted by copyright law.

Books may be purchased by contacting the publisher at:
CBW-LA Publications
P.O. Box 4376
Torrance, CA 90510
www.cbw-la.org
cbw-lapublications@cbw-la.org
(424) 261-2295

Cover design by: Garrigues Graphics
Edited by: Alana Garrigues and Nutschell Anne Windsor
Copyedited by: Erin Elizabeth Long
Book Formatting by: Morgan Media

Printed in the United States of America

ISBN-13: 978-0-9898787-9-1

First Edition
10 9 8 7 6 5 4 3 2 1

Story Sprouts

CBW-LA Writing Day I Exercises and Anthology
2013

A Collection of Writing Exercises
and the Resulting Creative Works of Fiction
by the Children's Book Writers of Los Angeles

Edited by:
Alana Garrigues
Nutschell Anne Windsor

CBW-LA Publications
Los Angeles

We dedicate this anthology to

aspiring authors,

writers at heart

and the inner child in all of us.

TABLE OF CONTENTS

Part I: On Writing

Section 1: Exercises

Section 2: Anthology Pieces

Poetry

Prose

Part II: Story Sprouts

Section 3: Exercises

Section 4: Anthology Pieces

Essay

Picture Book

Flash Fiction

Poetry

Appendices

Preface

Welcome!

You are about to enter a world of character and conflict, curiosity and quests, created by the minds of 19 published and aspiring children's book authors.

The stories you will read were created in a single day during a writing workshop hosted by the Children's Book Writers of Los Angeles. We have elected to include the workshop exercises and tips so that you may follow along with our authors from the comfort of your armchair.

The content is raw and inspired in the moment. As a result, some stories, though written by children's book authors, may be more suitable for a more mature audience. If you are a parent, please review the material first and then select the most appropriate stories to share with your little one.

Thank you for your support and readership!

Introduction

A Bit of History to Start Us Off

Before we proceed, let us answer a few questions for you. What is CBW-LA? How was the anthology created? And what can be found within these pages?

What is CBW-LA?

As an aspiring author, CBW-LA Founder Nutschell Anne Windsor knew that a solid writing community is an essential part of surviving the long and often lonely road to publication. So when she began her writing journey, she immediately went in search of a writing group that could not only give her the support and inspiration she needed to keep on writing, but also guide her with the knowledge she needed to pursue a writing career.

She found many wonderful groups, but none perfectly fit the schedule she had or the format she wanted. Nutschell wanted a group focused on children's book writing that met regularly near her home. She also wanted a writing group that provided affordable workshops and monthly writing classes.

Novelist Toni Morrison once said, "If there's a book you really want to read, but it hasn't been written yet, then you must write it." Inspired by Toni's insight, Nutschell thought the same rule should apply to writing groups. On June 30, 2010, she founded the Torrance Children's Book Writing Group on Meetup.com. Within a few days, eight other people had joined, and two weeks later,

Nutschell facilitated her first ever writing session with four other members.

From then on, Nutschell used her teaching experience to facilitate a variety of writing workshops and critique sessions. Through her networking efforts, Nutschell also began inviting published authors to conduct workshops, enabling her members to get the best education and insider knowledge while allowing authors to promote their work and get in touch with a new group of readers.

Attendance grew steadily, as did membership. In early 2011, the group's name was shortened to Torrance Children's Book Writers.

Nutschell established a leadership team to help her organize the group, assigning trusted members with unique roles and responsibilities. A full list of past board members is provided in the acknowledgements at the back of this book.

Currently, CBW-LA's Board of Directors include the following hard-working ladies: Nutschell Anne Windsor, Head Scribe (President); Lucy Ravitch, Second Scribe (Secretary); Tiffani Barth, Chamberlain (Treasurer); Alana Garrigues, Stationer (Publications Editor) and Angie Flores, Solicitor (Marketing Manager).

Also in 2012, the group officially changed its name to Children's Book Writers of Los Angeles, or CBW-LA for short. The group filed for a non-profit status, and in August of the same year, they received a 501 (c)(3) exemption status with the IRS and the State of California.

CBW-LA continues to educate and inspire writers in varying stages of their writing careers. The group has become known for its affordable, highly-rated and organized workshops, creative writing classes, and critique group sessions. Writing events are designed to accommodate all members' needs—whether they are beginning writers who want to know how to begin a novel, aspiring authors who wish to travel along the winding road to publication, or published authors who want to cross over from their current genre to children's book writing.

Nutschell started the group in the hopes of bringing together kindred spirits who would help each other grow and succeed as writers. Three years later, CBW-LA has surpassed all of her expectations. The small group has evolved into a thriving community with nearly 300 members. Most importantly, regular, active members have emerged as a driven bunch, determined not only to support each other's writing, but to help each other get published.

How Was the Anthology Started and What's Inside?

The Children's Book Writers of Los Angeles Writing Day Anthology was conceived during a board meeting in the fall of 2012. We wanted to find a way to support our authors on their journey to publication and infuse the year with creative energy. We also had a goal of modest fundraising for our club. With that in mind, we found delight in the idea of compiling an anthology of raw, in-the-moment writing.

Since our organization was founded on the principles of support and education, we felt a full day focused on the craft of writing, with the promise of a published piece by the end, fit the bill exactly.

Though the board members organized the workshop, it could not have happened without the men and women who participated in our first ever CBW-LA Writing Day Anthology. We were confident our idea was strong, but its success was entirely dependent on brave, creative writers willing to dedicate a single day to tap into ideas and expose vulnerabilities. We celebrate them for allowing us to share their work with the world through a final published piece.

Writers, we thank you. We applaud you. We admire you. We appreciate that you shared your time and your talent with all of us.

Readers, we now invite you on a journey. A peek into the exercises, discussions, and writing tips, tricks, and techniques that our writers experienced one June day in a library meeting room just south of the Los Angeles International Airport.

Please, join us. Try the exercises. See if the tips strike a chord. Play, have fun, and share with your friends.

Then read how our writers conquered the challenges and offer them your support. Each author submitted two pieces—one on writing and the second inspired by a photograph.

Check out the blogs and author sites listed in the Author Bios section, leave comments wherever you purchased the book, and keep your eyes and ears open for their names as they trickle into book stores with the stories and ideas they create on their own.

Welcome, and on with the stories!

Part I

On Writing

Section 1

Exercises

Section 1:

On Writing Exercises

Why Practice?

Writing is a craft. As such, it takes a great deal of precision and practice to achieve success and satisfaction.

Why practice? Why subject yourself to hours of writing and revision and idea creation?

Because practice makes perfect. We know this to be true about every skill. The only way that we can develop our writing skills—our craft—is to keep on practicing.

It doesn't mean that an author should hunker down and crank out novel after novel or picture book after picture book. To do so would not only prove repetitive and exhausting, but the author might also run the risk of sounding formulaic. While a successful author may ultimately publish many novels or picture books, that should not be the extent of his or her writing practice.

Practice that leads to inspiration and perfection, to mastering the craft, requires an author to dedicate time to honing the craft by focusing on the act of writing itself.

Often, authors and aspiring writers only engage with the manuscript, short story, or article they are working on. However, sometimes authors need a break from hard work. It is necessary to savor moments of writing just for the fun of composition. Or for the purpose of learning how to write better. Or to break through to new ideas and avenues of thought. Those are the times that creative writing exercises come in very handy.

The writing exercises included in this book—the exercises that inspired the stories you are about to read—are designed to help you, the writer, find your author voice and style.

The exercises are not overly complicated or time consuming. They were developed for shorter forms of literary works, such as essays, poems, and flash fiction. Descriptions of these formats, along with suggested techniques for working in each, are included in this book. Perhaps you want to approach an exercise using all three forms, one at a time, to see how your writing differs and which one best suits your voice.

The structure of this book mimics our Writing Day workshop. The first half focuses on warming up the mental muscles, followed by reflections and thoughts on writing in general. The second half showcases your writing chops and allows you to flex those literary muscles a little bit as you enjoy free reign over the topic of your choice, based on a photo prompt and assisted by a toolbox of story aids.

Exercise One: Warm Up
Right Brain Reigns - The Free Write

Any athlete will tell you that the first step to a successful workout is the warm-up. A few minutes to ease in, to get the muscles warm and pliable and the mind accustomed to a new activity. Writing is no different, and a little free writing to warm up does just the trick. To prepare for this first exercise, you will need:

*Laptop or pen(cil) and paper

*Timer

The Rules:

- Set a timer for five minutes.

- Write.

- No stopping or punctuation allowed.

Tips:

- Focus on the flow. Let your writing breathe. Do not think.

- Write whatever comes to mind. Do not worry about correct punctuation, grammar, or spelling. Let it be. Ignore the mistakes and go. If a topic appears, embrace it, but don't pick a topic to start.

- Write without stopping. At the end of the exercise, you should have a full block of text or a very long, rambling paragraph. No lists. Lists cut off your thoughts and force you to take pause.

- Do not stop writing until your timer goes off.
- Do not reread what you've written until time is up.

Why Does Free Writing Work?

Experimentation has shown that two different sides, or hemispheres, of the brain are responsible for different types of thinking. In very basic terms, we use our right brain for writing and our left brain for editing. Free writing allows us to tap into our right brain and shut out the internal editors. By forbidding a pause or punctuation, we incapacitate the bossy left brain and allow right brain to flow.

Much like physical exercise helps improve our body's health, writing exercises help us stretch our brain power and improve our mental health. By incorporating free writing into your schedule at least once a month, you will begin to notice improvements in your imaginative and descriptive writing powers.

But If It Looks Messy, What's The Point?

Idea creation.

Free writing is a great way to spark a new story idea or warm up your writing muscles before diving into your manuscript. You can also use free writing exercises to help you work out ideas when you're not sure of how a scene is supposed to unravel. Something else free writing is good for? Battling writer's block. Free write to look writer's block square in the face and beat it! The mindless act of free writing will help you release your creative side when confronted with a closed gate to Writerville.

Exercise Two: The Guided Free Write

Now that you've loosened a few cobwebs and warmed up, let's proceed with a guided exercise. You will need the same tools as the last exercise:

*Laptop or pen(cil) and paper

*Timer

This time, you will be asked to free write, but with a topic in mind.

The Rules:

- Set your timer for 10 minutes.
- Focus on the question: "How do I feel about writing?"
- Write.
- No stopping or punctuation allowed.

Tips:

- Using the question as a general guide, write continuously for ten minutes without stopping to edit or think.
- Allow your subconscious to take over and write down whatever pops into your head even if it doesn't make sense.
- Turn off your inner editor and let the words flow.

Exercise Three: Idea Extraction

With two exercises behind you, there are sure to be a few gems hiding in the mishmash that is a free write. Now it is time to find them. But before you do, here's what author Melissa Donovan has to say about the free writing process.

"Free writes can be used to bring creative, colorful language into prose. Strong images and rich language generates work that is more literary in nature and if done well, it's a lot more fun to read. It will help you generate words that show rather than tell and make you story or essay come alive more easily in a reader's mind."

–Melissa Donovan, Author of <u>101 Creative Writing Exercises (Adventures in Writing)</u>

The Rules:

- Read through the words that you've written for exercise two, the guided free write on writing.
- Underline or highlight words, phrases, and sentences that call out to you—the ones you find meaningful or that look and sound beautiful.

Hold on to them. They will be your inspiration for the next exercise.

Exercise Four: Putting It All Together

Did you find your magic, your inspiration? It's time to translate the world of writing into poetry or a brief piece of prose.

The Rules:

- Review the words, phrases, and sentences you underlined or highlighted in the last exercise.
- Decide if you'd like to compose a poem or prose.
- Set a timer for one hour to write and revise a poem or short essay (1,000 words max) on the topic of writing.

This is a good exercise to revisit periodically, as your reflections on writing will gradually evolve over time. You may uncover thoughts that were previously buried or discover new ideas. Many successful published authors have written books or magazine articles on the process of writing.

Now, without further adieu, the first pieces of our anthology. We share with you: **Writers on Writing**.

Section 2

Anthology Pieces

Poetry

Writer

By Abi Estrin

It is my secret, the soft pink inside of things,

gnarled toads in the riverbed,

dead or alive.

I am not afraid

to see (well, sometimes I am)

buried treasures in the mud,

willow trees swaying in the wind

beneath endless

clouds

under the sun.

I dig.

When things die, first they become smaller,

the physical form shrinks down

brittle, dissolving

into atoms and mud,

washed away in the summer rain.

I write.

I am still that kid in ripped jeans,

holes in her sneakers,

laughing

long-lost friends hiding behind a wheelbarrow,

running down the ravine,

playing in the salt mines,

catching fearless frogs and stones.

How can you sum up a lifetime in a word?

In a breath?

You are with me always in sun-soaked skies,

rolling in the too-long grass fields,

crunching leaves buried in moss-covered tree trunks,

chasing lizards

together

looking for insects

fossilized

in the amber

of memories.

I tell stories.

We write to remember the ghosts of our past,

the gleaming light of tomorrow.

We sing with words

to never forget.

I Am On The Path

By Lynne Southerland

I am on the path and it is glorious.

It takes me inside to the silent place that glues my life together.

It is solitary and private,

But desire longs to see others caressing what I have birthed.

I am on the path and it is glorious.

From the silence come words that can be shared through sight or voice,

Inner thoughts take shape into stories so different from my own,

But the core links me to you, like the universal DNA that binds us.

I am on the path and it is glorious.

Success comes each day as my characters grow into fully feeling beings.

Excitement swells when I envision others resting my book on their laps

as they sip tea or ride the metro or lie in bed.

I am on the path and it is glorious.

I release control and let the Muse flow through me with joy.

I play with the clay again and again to mold the ideas into a voice

that satisfies the spirit and nourishes the soul.

I am on the path and it is glorious.

A basketful of ideas awaits me when this book is done

I am grateful to have found this endless road of exploration

Elated to be gloriously incomplete

Writing vs. Reading

By Stacy Anderson

Writing without reading is the moon without the sun.

Reading without writing is watching without playing.

Writing for lovers. Reading for dreamers.

Two sides of the same coin.

One facing forward, one facing back.

Reading without writing is art without paintbrushes.

Writing without reading is painting without sight.

Reading is knowledge. Writing is power.

Two sides of the same coin.

One facing forward, one facing back.

Fly To Me

By Kristina F. Jordan, M.A.

Secret Lover

Hidden to myself

Unknowingly by Choice,

Buried in a watery casket

Of Doubt,

Fearing loss again

Of Pride,

Tears pushed down and overflowing

Inside the vaults of my child's heart

That longed—

Longed to be heard,

To be seen,

To be read.

Prison that holds me

In abeyance

Before the stark judgment

Of the empty page,

The empty book,

The empty space inside my creative groin

Longing to be filled,

To be heard,

To be seen,

To be read.

What terrifying emotions I would lay on the world

If I would.

What burdens, what traumas, what horrors I would unleash,

If I did.

Forget the sweetness, now here is the face of torture

If I wrote

What I think of,

And so I fear I'd

Harm the world with

My words.

Beyond the pale response I've encountered before,

From unwitting pawns in my own passion play

(When I pulled back from showing my passion),

Beyond the circles I've run trying to please

Those I thought were meant to be pleased,

Beyond the world I've only touched and

Have imagined beyond the world

Of my watery abyss,

Fly the skies of freedom I've yet to soar

For fear I would break the world,

Break my Self

I've worked so hard to construct,

And give others a chance once again

To break my heart.

My creative lover, still ever swimming
To the surface of my random thoughts,
Seeking permission to respond,
Respond, RESPOND
To its touch.

"Reach out, reach, yes Reach,
REACH
Beyond your fears," It sings
Like the Sirens' song
Luring me to dangerous reefs.

"You were born to fly
So why
Are you lanced to your
Rocky shores
By your
Own arms?"

"Come with me and I
Will lift you up
From the depths of your disappointment,
From the deep open trenches of your
Fear
Of rejection,
Once again."

"Swim with me and I will

Take you higher,

Higher than you've ever been.

And you will take me higher,

Soaring, lift me out and up,

Transforming my fins

Into feathers

Then Wings

Of Desire

Of Imagination

Of Permission

To Fly

Fly with your own Beautiful

Flights of Fancy,

Into Freedom,

Living Free

Living Happy

Living Life as a Writer,

LIVING

As you please."

As I please.

"And there,

You will be heard,

And there,

You will be seen, and finally,

There

You will be read."

"Kiss me.

Love me.

Feel me.

Be me.

Rise and Fly.

Rise and Fly.

Rise and Fly.

Fly To Me"

Books Written Rightly

By Glenn Jason Hanna

"What are you doing?" Randall asked Rich.

"I'm writing a story," Rich said.

"What's it about?" Randall inquired.

"It's about a guy who's dead."

"A guy who has died? That makes no sense.

Because the dead don't do a lot."

"It's not about him being dead.

How he died is the whole plot."

"Well, how did he die?" Randall asked Rich.

Rich shrugged because he didn't know.

"If your plot is what you don't know

The final prose's going to blow."

"Not so," Rich explained. "Plots are too hard

To conceive, to edit, to write.

Other things make a good book good

And those things I've nailed down tight.

Thousands of readers read my four blogs

On Twitter I've readers galore.

My marketing's ready to go.

I'm appearing on Channel Four.

You need a platform to sell a book.

To catch the public's eye.

How it's written, whether good or bad,

Has no bearing on what people buy.

So long as it's popular, people will read it

Even if the book's truly bad.

Who wants to miss out what's current and hot?

And be thought of as clueless and sad?"

Rich smiled and smiled and finished his prose.

Randall left, confused and upset.

"To write gibberish just to get paid

Would leave me filled with regret."

Randall gave thought about what he should do.

"I could try to talk to Rich,

To get him to write a book that's good,

To flip on his creative switch.

Or steal his prose and throw it away,

Or just punch him in the nose."

Randall gave thought to all of those options.

But none of those choices he chose.

"Books written rightly—if they're to be,

Then I have to write them," he said.

So he sat down to write, and the first thing he thought

Was how a dead guy winded up dead.

Prose

The Writer

By Tiffani Barth

I wrote my first story when I was five, a picture book called *Ellie Comes Home*. Ellie was a little girl, like me, who was disappointed to receive no gifts for her birthday. Instead she only got a card. She soon learned just how special that card actually was when she found herself inside the picture on the front and immersed in a land of fairies, of which she was a queen.

From the time I wrote *Ellie Comes Home*, my love for stories grew, and so did my imagination. In fifth grade, I received a special award from my principal for breaking the record for the most books ever read by a student in one school year. I loved to read anything that would take me away on a magical journey somewhere away from the life that I considered mundane. I dreamed of one day going on my own adventures and would compose secretive plans for my prospective journeys. These plans turned into stories, and soon, writing became an outlet for those dreams. When written as a narrative, they became real to me, even if they were happening to fictional characters.

My love for words started early, in the days before kindergarten and *Ellie*, when my mother would sit down with me and teach me how to put my favorite ABC song to work. I remember how grown up I felt when I started to be able to read the words on road signs and would proudly blurt them out to my parents and friends. I didn't stop there. Now that I could read like an adult, I wanted to write like one too. I begged my mother to teach me cursive and would spend hours creating loop-de-loop letters with my pen, loving the windy flow of ink on paper.

Many young people spend a lot of time searching for their calling. They browse career fairs, switch college majors, counsel with academic advisors, trying to find the best course for them. This was something I never had to do. I always knew what I wanted to be. I might travel many different roads to get there, but I would never stop until I was worthy of the title of writer.

Today, the prospect of writing is what gets me up in the morning. It's what I think about as I'm falling asleep at night. A friend once asked me if I'd regret all the hours—months, years—and missed summer vacations I'd spent writing if I ended up never getting published. I told her no. Writing is what gives me hope and keeps me going every day. It's what brings color into my otherwise black and white world. It allows me to escape to another place and become someone else for a time, all the while revealing deep truths about myself. Every story I create is, in a way, a journal for my emotions and deepest fears and desires. It's my passion, it's my lifestyle, and it's my identity. I am very grateful to be a writer.

The Pit

By Cacy Duncan

The pit of quicksand in her backyard grew larger and larger as she watched with trepidation from behind the screen door.

The water and sand had mixed perfectly, and it was her fault. She didn't think it would work. She was only eight years old, after all. What did she know about mad science and reforming nature to her will?

But look at it now. It was no longer her little homemade pit of quicksand. It was a creature with its own will...and out of her control.

There must have been something buried under the yard. A drum of radioactive material, maybe. Or a magical talisman that had been down there long before the suburb was built. Whatever caused this didn't matter. The damage was already done.

The creature reached a wet, sloshing arm out from the muck. Then another. It pulled itself upward and blinked, opening three yellow, glowing eyes.

As she stared, awestruck, through the screen door, the quicksand creature took its first step toward the house.

Then a second.

She leapt out of her stupor and hurried to her bedroom, wiping the mud off her hands as she ran. She had to do something about this, and she knew exactly what that was.

But first she needed...she needed...

There it was!

Paper and a pencil.

She threw herself onto her bed, scribbling frantically as she gave the rampaging creature in her imagination life on the page.

Come Out and Play

By Diane H. Fisk

"Tilly, come out and play with me," yelled Benjamin outside her window. "It's a bright, sunny day, and the birds are singing so beautifully this morning."

Tilly lifted her window and breathed in the cool, fresh air.

What a wonderful day, she thought to herself.

Then she looked over at her desk. Her notebook was wide open to a story she had started last night. Tilly felt torn. Should she go out and play with Benjamin or finish the story she had started? What to do?

Just as she started to say yes to Benjamin, Jack, a character in her story, jumped right out of her notebook and onto the floor!

Tilly jumped back and rubbed her eyes. Jack, the rabbit in her story, was standing right in front of her!

"No time to play," Jack said. "You need to finish your story right this minute! All of your friends in your story are waiting to find out what to do. You need to write it."

"Are you real? Really for real?" Tilly asked.

"I'm as real as you make me," Jack replied.

"Wow. This is so cool!" said Tilly.

Tilly yelled out her window to Benjamin.

"Sorry. I can't come and play today. I've got to finish writing my story. My friends are all waiting on me!" she said.

"What do you mean, all your friends are waiting on you?" he asked.

"No time to explain," Tilly said as she closed her window.

Benjamin turned and walked down the hill.

"I thought I was her best friend," he whispered.

Tilly went to her desk and sat down. Other character friends in her story were walking around on her pages, looking up at her. There was a toad, a frog, and a fish.

"Please, tell us what to do," they begged.

"My goodness! I didn't realize how important I am."

Tilly started writing. As she did, all her characters did exactly what she told them to do.

"This is so much fun!" she said. "I love to write. I can create anything I want on these pages, and all my friends are here with me!"

So, as Tilly wrote and wrote, her story came to life. When she was finished she read it to her mother. Her mother said it was the most wonderful story she had ever heard because it seemed that her characters came to life and were so real.

Moved by the Muse

By Angie Flores

Clear your mind, girl. Will you write?

The room is quiet, dim. Her relaxation candle burns with jasmine, flickering, beckoning her ideas to manifest. Finally, she is gifted a moment of freedom from the blessings of being needed. The sound of her kids arguing downstairs has turned into white noise as she settles in.

She starts.

I am a writer who...that...which...

Damn. A block.

Did my husband feed the kids? Will my boys get to practice on time?

Procrastination is holding her hand.

How to start? How to start?

Her mind is filled with the clutter that forms from all the minute-to-minute details of being a mom, a wife, and just trying to find herself.

Self-doubt blankets her with fear.

Am I capable of doing this?

Thoughts of her lack of majoring in English are haunting her confidence. A rebel in discipline, and the absence of motivation, have anchored her for so long, but now she realizes she has a void to fill. The casual use of her street slang won't cut it with an editor or agent unless she attaches it to a character.

A character? A boy? A dog who talks? A boy who talks to dogs?

Holy crap! I forgot to defrost the chicken! Chicken? How can I write

39

with chicken on my mind?!

A strong inhale of air fills her lungs as she exhales the pressures of responsibility.

Think, girl. This can't be that hard. You got this. Think!

This is what she has always wanted to do. Yet the self-doubt and the assumption of weak skills portray it as an incapable goal.

Like a kid reaching for a cookie jar on the top shelf, her will stretches. Will she ever get there? As she attempts to dilute her stress with the scent of jasmine, her eyes cloud with the tears of surrender.

Maybe this isn't for her. As her mind starts to drift she feels the warmth of a hug pulling her in.

The memory of her grandma embraces her heart as she looks into the mirror on her makeshift desk, which doubles as her dresser. The purr of her grandma's voice fills her ears and caresses her heart.

"It's all in your noggin dear. Don't overthink this. Just write what you know and the rest will come."

A tear splashes onto the hand that has been paralyzed on the keyboard, releasing the tension and awakening the mind.

Straightening up and smiling at her reflection, she cautiously accepts the introduction of a new confidence.

Her grandma is her muse, a writer herself.

With a nod of concurrence, she knows what to do. Cracking her knuckles and stretching her arms, she takes a deep breath, wiggles her fingers, and starts her journey.

I am a mom who writes.

Solitary Encounters

By Alana Garrigues

I write at night, when the world around me sits in silence. With my husband and children nestled soundly into their beds, drifting off into dreamland, I make myself a cup of tea, sit at the computer, and attempt to open the elusive writer's vein.

When I am lucky, inspiration strikes early and the pages flow, words and phrases dancing on the page, lingering here, hopping there, twisting and turning and building, finally set free from the constant revision in my head. Other nights, feeling particularly creative but noncommittal, I shun the staccato tap tap tap of the keyboard and pull open a notebook with a nice sharp pencil to jot down "big ideas," seeds that may one day turn into first pages and finished drafts. Most nights, facing an impending deadline, I waste time tinkering on social media and email correspondence before settling in to the writer's rhythm.

And though I prefer to write in silence, my nights at the keyboard are far from lonely.

Every night, sitting alone at my desk, I am visited by solitary encounters, conversations that live forever in my mind, real or imagined, with those who drove me to this crazy, vulnerable, exciting world of writing. They are the authors I admire, the friends and family I love, the mentors who believed in me. When I am stuck, they sit beside me and push me forward. These solitary encounters in the dead of night bring smiles, laughter, bravery, melancholy, inspiration. Who are these solitary encounters, and what do they bring me?

There is always my paternal grandfather, my Grandpa Julius. By most modern American standards, Grandpa Julius would not be considered an educated man. At 15 years old, he left high school to earn a living, taking responsibility for his parents and brothers' well-being. By the time he met my Grandma, he'd been working for a decade. Grandpa sometimes mispronounced words, ordering a glass of muhr-lot (merlot).

Despite his lack of a diploma, my grandfather was one of the smartest, most well-read men I have ever met. He would relate the history of Portland from its early days to the day he died, describing the circumstances that led to the infrastructure and local politics of a big city with small town heart. He could pull up sports statistics from nearly any team sport from memory. And he read the newspaper, faithfully, front to back, every day. Always with a smile and a little twinkle in his eye. Always looking for bias and content, impressed when he found none. He sought straight facts in the local paper for his news and entertainment, and he soaked up every word.

Today, I am a journalist. He didn't live to see it. It was a career I secretly dreamed of but never pursued until an opportunity dropped into my lap by chance. On the day he died, there was no way that my grandpa could have known that 30 months later his first grandchild would be one of the people creating the type of content he read his entire life.

Every article that I write, I write with my Grandpa Julius in mind, taking care to mix historical and cultural context with unbiased reporting and a peek into all sides of a single story. Through my Grandpa, I am reminded that the stories I tell are not my own. I am merely the caretaker and the conduit of the stories of others. My Grandpa passed away two years before I started writing for the paper, but I have no doubt he would have been the proudest, reading and clipping all my articles for safekeeping. With my Grandma encouraging me to follow my heart and stay true and honest to myself along the way. Reading each article through their eyes gives me the confidence and love to push forward.

Then there are the others. Less frequent, perhaps, less personal, certainly, but always inspirational and reassuring.

For organization and the ability to support a hypothesis, there is my high school English teacher, a man who taught at Purdue and a lone atheist in a Catholic high school. He taught me that no argument is balanced unless the opposing argument is recognized, considered, and then addressed directly. An opinion lacks merit and conviction without opposition.

I call on my babysitter Heather for whimsy and good storytelling. A girl who at the age of 10 was trusted to care for countless children, my sister and I included, and did so with a level of creativity and grace that I have not seen before or since in any caretaker. She arrived at my house with bags full of books that she had written, bound, and illustrated—classic fairy tales with her own little twist or fresh, modern dialogue. Heather inspired a six-year-old me to spend hours performing in my living room, acting out the stories that she wrote, anxious to find out when my parents would leave for their next date so I could take the stage in front of the fireplace.

When I feel afraid that I need to simplify my writing and limit myself to mono- or disyllabic words to satisfy a younger audience, I smile at A.A. Milne and his complicated themes and rich language. Through his characters and their simple stories, Milne showed that children have the ability to learn and absorb language through context without being inundated with rules and explanations. When I want to remind myself that pigeonholes can be smashed, I call on Roald Dahl who successfully broke out of the genre he was first published in and wrote for children and adults alike, proof that an author with talent, and most of all perseverance, who knows the audience for each story can do it.

Finally, when I feel as though I can't tell a tale, I remember Tim Gillespie, my middle school writing teacher who worked with a handful of students on a weekly basis up in the alcove of our school library. Excused from regular class time, the five of us would bring our latest stories for what I now know to be a critique session, reading our work aloud and commenting on one another's progress. For as I looked around and saw people who could create a story out of nothing, I returned to themes that were familiar to me—everyday activities, real friendships—and wove them into my stories. I felt incredibly lacking in creativity, but Mr. Gillespie didn't see that. He saw some sort of raw talent in what I now know to be the seed of creative nonfiction, my preferred genre. And the fact that he was not surprised when he found out 20 years later that I was writing, the fact that he remembered my stories after two decades, gives me courage to know that someone believed in me from the start. It reassures me that I was meant to be a writer.

These are the people who speak to me in the quiet of the night, who push me to write better, and to trust my instincts. These are the conversations I cherish.

Who are your solitary encounters, the silent cheerleaders and gentle critics, pushing you to be a better you?

My Two Cents: From Story Idea to Submission

By Lucy Ravitch

I don't know about you, but writing is part of the roller coaster of life. It takes determination and grit. When reading a good book, you may think, I can do that, but when you try, you find that the words don't flow or the story isn't captivating. Here is how I do it—and if I can do it, so can you!

First of all, you should know a little bit about me. I'm a mother of five kids—yes, five—all age 12 and under. My husband is away at work 10-11 hours each day Monday through Friday as I take kids back and forth to school, doctor appointments, swim classes, and tutoring. I don't always have time to write, let alone sit down and eat most days. Luckily, I make time to think of ideas and write picture books whenever I can. My normal writing time comes late at night before bed, in the middle of the night after feeding the baby, or in the wee hours of the morning.

You may wonder what to write about. I believe everyone has a creative side to them. For some it comes easier than others, but if you have determination, you can do it. My mind is constantly thinking. I feel very blessed to be a creative person, always thinking of how to solve problems and organize things. I may have a topic or idea for a book, but the way to write that story or book comes later. For example, I knew I wanted to write a decimals book for almost a year and a half before the idea of how to weave it into a story came at three o'clock early one morning. I typed the storyline into my laptop and went back to bed.

But how do you write the book? It starts with an idea. Hopefully you know what form of writing you like to write— picture books, novels, easy readers, middle grade, etc. There are ideas for stories all around. I get most of my ideas from educational topics. I then take a topic and come up with a way to teach that idea with a story or concept.

Once you have that idea and how the story will go, the most important step begins—you write it down! Don't worry if it doesn't sound great; you have completed your rough draft. That is what it is going to be—rough.

With the rough draft, you can do a quick revision to check for grammar, spelling, and punctuation mistakes, but then I recommend you put it away. Hide it, even. (But do remember where you put it.) After a week or two, look at it again and revise. Set a time limit for yourself so you don't end up over-revising. Then put it away one more time and wait at least another week. Revise again. Now it will most likely be ready for outside eyes to see it.

You may be wondering, do I really need to wait so long before sharing it?

It will be in your best interest to have revised it at least two times before showing your work to others. Also, when I say "show it to others," I am not talking about your nephew and his neighbor friend. I mean other writers.

I enjoy taking my writing to the online critique group I normally exchange my work with. After they have given their critique, I may make changes right away if I like them, but then I put it away again.

Once I bring the manuscript out a week or two later, I go over all the comments and critiques that I couldn't bear to listen to at first. I take what I think would help my work and apply it. Other comments I brush aside, knowing that I don't have to accommodate other's opinions in my work.

What next? I take the revised manuscript to another group of critique partners at an event of some sort. These are people that haven't seen my work before. This gives new eyes on my work and another chance to see how it is perceived.

Once again, I put the work aside with all the comments and revise a week or two later. Distance between revisions helps me see more of what the critique partner meant. Again, sometimes I end up tweaking part of the manuscript and other times I just ignore the feedback.

Remember to be true to yourself and what you want your work to be like.

Once I feel it is ready and polished, I go online and to writing events to try to find potential agents and editors who take my sort of work. Here is where the determination and grit comes in. You will get rejected. It happens to the best of the best, but your work will get the attention it deserves if you continue to persevere.

While waiting for letters and responses about your manuscript, keep writing and keep your ideas flowing for other works. In time, success will come.

Is it really worth all the work?

That is a question you have to ask yourself.

What do you want?

For me, writing is part of my life. It is a way for me to release my inner creative side. I am excited to share it with the world. I have confidence that my work will be available soon and that children and adults will enjoy my work. It has taken years of refining, but it has only gotten better over that time. When rejections come, I take them and keep going. A positive attitude is key, and persistence is critically important.

I wish you all the best of luck in your writing journey!

Constant Companion

By Donna Marie Robb

Writing has been my companion for as far back as I can remember. When I was a toddler, I used to tell myself stories aloud and sketch primitive pictures of the characters that invaded my mind.

When I started first grade, my mom enrolled me in piano lessons. I didn't enjoy them all that much, but they inspired me to create my own world, "Music Land," where all the characters were musical notes. These stories were mostly rehashes of popular fairy tales such as Cinderella, set in my special land. I even made little books from small scraps of paper that my dad stapled together, complete with sketched crayon illustrations.

I started my first novel at sixteen, which took place in the distant future. I entered it in an international contest for teen writers. My novel didn't win, but I was inspired to keep writing, eventually majoring in creative writing as an undergraduate in college.

I continue to write today, decades later.

My feelings about it are often mixed and muddled. Sometimes it's a gentle lover that fills me with the deepest comfort. Those are the times when I curl up on the couch and allow my imagination to go wild. Anything is possible when I write—exotic new worlds replete with life pop into existence, where people can fly and magic is real. It is easy to get lost in these make-believe places as the mundane world fades into the background, at least for a while. This has brought me tidbits of success in the form of stories accepted for magazines and the occasional, "I love what you wrote!"

But writing has also been a fickle friend that has brought its share of disappointments—impersonal form rejections, unanswered emails, drenched hopes. These experiences have, at times, clogged my brain with that dreaded malady called "writer's block." Those are the times when I'd rather do anything instead of write, whether it's watching a movie I've seen many times before or escaping into a long nap.

Yes, writing is my close companion, a life-long relationship. We have our troubles, but then there are the blissfully good times that make it all worthwhile. We have been together for a long, long time. Occasionally we need a break from one another but, in the end, we are in it for the long haul.

The Senses of Writing

By Diane Sepulveda Robinson

Putting that first shaky step of a thousand steps, along a long, mysterious and unknown path into the exciting journey of writing, has led into a world of human senses we take for granted. The awakening feelings of rousing, stimulating, inspiring and stirring were introduced to my creative right brain.

Touch

In other words, let us discuss the sense of touch in the feeling of writing. Can you feel the soft material when touching a baby blanket? I remember bathing my baby daughter and putting the pink, fluffy blanket around her tiny body. Words of love, joy and happiness express the touch of my hands against her soft skin.

See

How do you feel about the sense of sight when you see your baby's tiny fingers, feet and hands? Do you see them wriggling out of the soft and velvety pink blanket, trying to be free from it?

Smell

Can you smell that whiff of the traditional baby powder? A scent that can be elegantly described as a fragrant bouquet of love?

Hear

How powerful is the sense of sound when you hear your baby's first cries being brought into a world surrounded by beauty, nature and strange humans in white uniforms? How powerful to hear your baby laughing and screaming for joy when changing a (stinky) diaper? Or just picking your baby up to hear such joy?

Harmonize

How appealing is it when your senses can be expressed into potent and intoxicating writings of the joy, love, and happiness of early parenthood?

You can recall, perhaps, your early childhood years. What did it feel like when you touched your first pet? Was it soft, smooth, slimy, big, small, smelly, or just did it just lay there like a pet rock?

Or perhaps you can recall the times when you fell down and mom or dad picked you up to feel that you were okay. Do you remember the sudden spark of pain and the soft touch of your mom or dad kissing it and wrapping a sticky Band-Aid around it? Did your senses tell you it was going to be all right, that soon you could go back to hearing the sounds of the playground, the touch of the hard metal of the see-saw, the smell of hot dogs cooking in the park, and the noise of your playmates yelling around you?

Ahh, the sweet senses that can be brought back in simple words of intoxicating descriptions.

It is a language of my heart and soul.

On the Road to a Masterpiece

By Nora Rodriguez

Writing has always been a form of relief for me.

I first started scribbling as a teenager. My friend Ruth and I would pick topics to write about, and then we'd share them with each other. We were each other's first audience. As I got older, my writing deviated from puppy love poems and topics selected by my friend into more serious matters. I continued to write, but I used it more as an outlet for my frustrations.

While in college, I started keeping a journal as part of a class assignment. It was just a regular notebook, but it was my therapy. In the notebook, I would write all my complaints, fears, and furies, along with any good events that happened. I would always feel much better after I wrote things down. However, this caused me to stop sharing my writing with others for fear of what they would say or think. I wasn't writing anything insulting or horrendous, but I still didn't want others to know my true feelings. Pen and paper had become my outlet. They were a pair of ears with no eyes to see me, nor a nose to smell my feelings, and no mouth to criticize me with. Writing was also an outlet for my creative ideas. If something inspired me, I wrote about it, usually in the same notebook I use for therapy writing.

I still don't share it with others though. I have become sort of like a "lone writer." I write by myself and for myself. But I hope that one day I do write a piece of work worthy of publication and being shared with the world. Then someone will find all those writings and see that even though I was just "de-stressing" at the time it was written, I was practicing to write a masterpiece!

The Rains of North Queensland

By Lissa Ross

The wind whistled through the airy fisherman's shack on the edge of a deserted beach in Northern Queensland, Australia. Sitting at an old computer in the corner of the room was an older woman, staring out to sea. She watched the storm clouds building in the distance.

The memories came flooding back as she typed, like the flood waters that came every year in the rainy season. The stories she'd heard since childhood of torrential rain and the flooded creeks in the outback, where people drowned or were stranded for days and sometimes weeks on one side, with no way of moving until the rain had stopped and the creeks went down.

There was the story of her grandmother, trying to get back to the family cattle station during the rains. When the creek flooded its banks and kept her captive for three days, the stockmen came looking for her on horseback. Much to her horror, they told her that her only option was to swim across the flooded creek on the back of the quiet-tempered old mare they had brought with them.

Having never ridden a horse, let alone having to swim across a raging river on one, it must have been a terrifying ordeal. Her grandmother often laughed until tears streamed down her face when she told the story of how she held on tightly to the horse's mane, terrified of drowning because she had never learned to swim.

So she sat and wrote about the history of her family.

The original pioneers who had settled in the area three

generations ago, arriving on horses and wagons to settle in and unknown land. A life full of hardship and simple joy.

She wondered about her family history and if those brave souls were looking down from the other side.

A breeze blew through the room.

What would they like her to say?

Finding Inspiration at the Festival of Books

By Christal Terry

The L.A. Times Festival of Books was at the beautiful and normally serene University of Southern California. On this day, it seemed particularly chaotic and frustrating, so much so that I could barely appreciate the stunning architecture and meticulous landscaping.

I was there with my son and nephew, both only seven years old.

One of the things I remember about it was the heat and the exhaustion from all the walking. It felt like we'd spent hours trying to find the Target Children's Stage, stopping several times to look at maps and ask for information.

I kept thinking about the small legs and extreme patience of my companions. Maybe it was a mistake to drag them here with me, I thought. After all, as much as I wanted them to share my love of books, I was also there as a writer. I wanted to learn what a book festival was all about and what I could expect as an aspiring author.

I still call myself that, an aspiring author. I've written two books that would now be covered in cobwebs if it were possible for them to get dusty in my word processor.

After a year and a half, all I'd done to publish my work was attend critique sessions hosted by the Children's Book Writers of Los Angeles. I'd also read a book called The Complete Idiot's Guide to Publishing Children's Books, but I was no closer to publishing my stories than the day I finished writing them. There had been no query letters, no knocking down the doors of agents or publishers. Just a hope and a dream. Or more like a wing and a prayer, and a lot of hot air. I was still doing what I like to call "background work," better known as foot shuffling and procrastination to the layman.

In spite of that, there I was at the Festival of Books, doing more of my "background work" and practically torturing two innocent children. Though I saw it as torture, the children scarcely had a complaint. Maybe they were just glad to be out of the house, or maybe, just maybe, they understood what all the hubbub was about. I was touched at the end of the day when these two small children had somehow rekindled my passion for writing...just by being themselves.

After a reading and Q&A session by Jon Klassen, bestselling children's book author of *This Is Not My Hat* and *I Want My Hat Back*, I wanted to get a book as a souvenir for my son. I spent what little money I had on it. My son insisted we wait in an incredibly long line so that he could meet the author and get his autograph. Though it had been a long day, I was so impressed by his request that I was happy to oblige.

After waiting an hour in the blazing hot sun, it was finally our turn to greet Jon Klassen. I had written down what I'd like to be inscribed on the book—*To Cayne, may you have a lifelong love of books.* There we were, my son, my nephew, and I, standing in front of this beaming author who I imagined was tired after a reading, a Q&A session, and what seemed like hundreds of signatures. He didn't show it, though. He was every bit as friendly and as excited to be there as my son and nephew.

I remember my nephew asking him, "Where did a bear get a hat in the first place?"

I chuckled at the innocence and sweetness of the question. The author smiled widely and responded, "You know, I don't know...I think maybe he found it."

Then he signed our book and said simply, "You guys have been great, thank you so much for being here."

He meant it, too. I could tell he loved children and loved what he did. That was what it was about. Not financial gain, not paying the bills, but being a part of something bigger —inspiring a love of books and, in turn, being inspired by the children who love them.

Baseball Revelations

By Kathryn Thornton

-Baseball Diamond-

It is February, and here I am again, sitting on a cold metal bleacher while my six-year-old son has baseball practice. I hate baseball. Two practices a week and two games a week. Who has that kind of time to waste?

Two weeks of practice and I am already running the "I hate baseball" mantra through my head daily.

Why is this season so much more taxing? I think. *We barely won any games last year. This season has to be better.*

Great. My phone is dead. What am I going to do for two hours?

-Home-

"Hi honey," my husband of 20 years says as he saunters in from work. "Where's dinner?"

"Oh. You can make yourself a sandwich or something."

I have never told my husband to make his own meal. Right now I just wish he would leave me alone.

"What about the kids?"

"I fed them." *Can't he see that I am busy?*

"What are you doing?" he asks incredulously.

"It's amazing. I started writing at practice three hours ago. The story is just flowing out of me and I feel so alive, so happy. I can't stop."

I turn back to my half-full notebook and scrawl the words as fast as I can to keep pace with my thoughts. The story keeps evolving, and, surprisingly, the pieces are all working together. The story organically grows as I allow myself the freedom to let it flow.

-Mid-Season-

"You haven't been complaining about baseball practice," my husband observes. "Are you beginning to like the sport now that we are halfway through the season?"

No. But I covet those two-hour practices twice a week as if they are manna from heaven. I purchased a laptop, and my novel consumes all my thoughts. Practice always ends too soon and I must return to my everyday responsibilities.

"You have been the happiest I have ever seen during a baseball season," my husband quips. "It must be the winning season we are having. This is the best team we've had yet!"

"It has nothing to do with baseball. I know that Andrew is having a great season, but I am happy because of my writing."

I can't contain my smile as I think of my newfound love.

"This is going to stop after baseball season, right?"

"No. I am happy because I write. Why would you want me to stop? I didn't realize it but I felt stagnant before and now...now I feel whole."

-Post-Season-

I still hate baseball. My son's team lost only two out of 19 games, and he is more in love with it than ever. Still, I don't know which of us is looking forward to the start of the next season more.

I completed my first novel this season. I expect by the start of the next season I will have my second novel well underway and hope to finish it before his season is done.

Maybe I'll even be published by then.

Curse of Apollo

By Cameron Ulyate

"Apollo, what does it mean to be a writer?"

Apollo chuckled. "You've traveled all this way to meet a Greek god and this is your question."

The man who had asked the question stood still, second-guessing himself and whether his adventure up the frosty mountain was worth it.

A cup of tea appeared on Apollo's golden throne. Apollo stared at the man and took a deep breath.

"In writing there are no rules for what you're allowed to imagine. If you want to write a story about a king or queen trapped in a spaceship, go ahead. If your story calls for an adventure with wizard-pirates finding magical buried treasure, go ahead."

"But Apollo, what if I'm not the best speller and my paper is littered with mistakes?" the man asked.

"So what? Mistakes and spelling can always be fixed, but not the adventures wandering through your mind; they are the most important. Those adventures want to come out. First, write your adventure and bring your characters and world out from your mind and onto the page. Editing comes later."

"But, Apollo, what if I do write and no one wants to read my work?"

"You can't live with that doubt. Some people may want to read your writing; others may not. However, think of your stories as a ticket to immortality. I know I do. I feel that writing allows the writer to not just enter into their own world, but to bring the reader along with them. People who read your writing don't just see how well you tell a story. They get to look into your thoughts and ideas, even if you've been gone for a hundred years. It's a gateway into your mind.

"I'll use myself as an example—you know, since I'm a god and everything. If people didn't tell stories about me, do you think I would continue to exist? The answer is most likely not. Telling stories about us gods keeps us alive because people get a chance to think about us, which gives us power. Your characters may or may not exist in real life, but when you write about them, they can come alive. People may even want to write adventures using your characters as fan-fiction."

The man grabbed hold of his bag and walked down the topaz stairs. He turned to Apollo.

"I think I understand what you're saying. I just need to write and not worry about all the minor details," he said.

Apollo laughed. "Yes. And no matter what you write in this world, just make sure it's what makes you happy."

Apollo watched the man leave. *A few more left and then Zeus will let me return.*

A microphone appeared in Apollo's other hand. Into the microphone he spoke, "Now serving guest 292!"

A woman approached. Apollo smiled. "What can I do for you?"

The Author Who Changed the World

By Nutschell Anne Windsor

I want to be exactly like J.K. Rowling. But not for the reasons you might think.

Sure, it would be nice to earn millions of dollars, have movies made based on my books, and even get a theme park built around my stories. But that's just icing on the cake, as they say.

J.K. Rowling changed the world forever when she wrote *Harry Potter*. And not just because she contributed new words like "muggle" to our vocabulary.

J.K. Rowling's works have triggered a tsunami of creativity affecting all forms of media. Fan fiction based on her characters has flooded various blogs and online sites, wizard rock has invaded the music scene, and movie adaptations of her books have become major blockbusters—a far cry from where we were creatively a mere decade ago.

When I was growing up, there weren't many books with main characters I could easily relate to. Most of the characters I read about were either younger or older than I was. And if I wanted to read a good fantasy book, I'd have to go into the adult section to find one.

J.K. Rowling changed all that by showing the publishing industry that there was money to be made in children's books, thereby ushering in the golden age of children's literature.

Harry Potter flung the doors of imagination wide open, inspiring a whole new breed of children's book authors to create timeless stories that appeal to children and adults alike.

Harry Potter made reading cool again. Children who normally ignored anything that didn't involve technology turned into avid bookworms. They set aside their video game consoles and computers so they could sit down and read hundreds of pages about the boy who went to Hogwarts. Once these children became involved with Harry and his story, their literary cravings never went away. The children who first picked up the books out of curiosity soon found themselves searching for new stories to fill the void left behind by *Harry Potter* and the fight for literacy was won.

Even adults who thought they were too old for whimsy and fantasy began to remember their love of good stories. *Harry Potter* gave them a magical world to escape their adult woes for a while, and much like a time machine, the stories gave them a way to relive the joys of childhood once more.

Most importantly, J.K. Rowling proved that great stories transcend all social barriers. She brought people from all over the world together with the power of her ideas alone. Race, age, gender, and nationality all disappeared when everyone started rooting for Harry and his friends. She shaped a generation of children who grew up believing that friendship, loyalty, and courage are desirable traits. That as long as you don't give up, you can achieve anything. That good always triumphs over evil. And that love conquers all.

J.K. Rowling did all this, not by creating a literary masterpiece, but by writing a story that everyone could easily understand. Her words were powerful in their simplicity, reaching the minds and hearts of even the youngest of readers.

Yes, I want to be the next J.K. Rowling. I want to be an author who changes the world.

I want to create unforgettable characters who are good role models for children. I want to weave memorable plots that buzz in readers' minds long after they've put the book away. I want to come up with dialogue that can start a discussion anywhere, that will be quoted time and again. I want to build worlds that invite readers to widen their imaginations and challenge them to open up to new experiences. I want to write a story that will inspire millions to remake the world around them and change it for the better.

Most of all, I want to write a story that can transform at least one person's life.

If I can make one child feel less alone—if I can make him or her realize that magic lives in our hearts—if I can make him believe in himself and the power of his dreams, then I know I will have changed the world. Just like J.K. Rowling.

Part II

Story Sprouts

Section 3

Exercises

Section 3:

Story Sprouts Exercises

Once the CBW-LA Writing Day workshop attendees completed their writing entries and enjoyed a pause for socializing and refreshments, we moved on to part two: writing a story, complete with a character, conflict, beginning, middle, and end. All within three hours from idea generation through submittal.

Realizing just how tall the order was, we were ready with props, ideas, and lots of tips and support.

Where Does a Story Originate?

Writing is a perfect example of life imitates art imitates life. The two work hand in hand. We write because we are alive; life itself inspires the writer. For the extroverts among us, that may mean big adventures and wild experiences. For the introverts, the nuance of inner life, the life in our minds, may be the primary inspiration.

With a mix of fiction and nonfiction writers in our midst, it was important to discuss how ideas could truly come from anywhere.

So, where does a story come from? We identified three primary sources, all of them imminently accessible to all writers, regardless of genre, audience, ability, or location.

Here they are:

- The Five Senses
- Our Experiences
- Feelings and Emotions

The Five Senses

Stories are hiding in every experience of our senses.

Need a reminder of the five senses?

- See
- Smell
- Taste
- Touch
- Hear

Most of us rely most on what we see, but different writers use their different senses to communicate. Food writers would be lost without their sense of taste, and music critics could not compose without their sense of hearing.

Sometimes we gain story ideas in the first person, observing the world before us in the moment. As writers, we carefully watch human interactions, particularly those involving passion or discord, and create stories in our minds that focus on characters and conflicts and imagined dialogues. We look at people and places differently, drawing meaning and reading between the lines.

That which we see—a mountain capped with snow, a budding flower, a storm, a kite festival, live theater—inspires.

That which we hear—a crowing peacock, the cracking jolt of an earthquake, the cacophony of a busy intersection, a soothing melody, raindrops on the rooftop—inspires.

That which we taste—the pursing power of a lemon wedge, the heat of a jalapeno, a bite of decadent molten chocolate cake drizzled with a raspberry glaze, the salt of a potato chip—inspires.

That which we smell—the scent of lavender, the fragrance of the dewy grass following a night of rain, kitchen spices or baked bread signaling a favorite family recipe, even the stench of a back street alley in a big city—inspires.

That which we touch—a soft and well-loved blanket, a smooth pebble, the bristling face of a wild animal, our grandparent's wrinkled hands—inspires.

At times, our five senses trigger an original story. Other times, that which we see, hear, smell, taste and touch weaves its way into the stories we write and edit.

We can also find inspiration for material from other people's experiences and creations. We may visit a gallery and see a photograph or a painting that clicks on a story in our mind. "The Girl with the Pearl Earring," painted by Johannes Vermeer, inspired a widely circulated novel by Tracy Chevalier. Television news coverage is rife with story material for fiction and nonfiction writers alike, as is traditional media in the form of newspaper and magazine articles. Woody Allen once shared during a television interview that he collects newspaper clippings—odd headlines and stories that catch his eye—and stores them in a drawer for dry days.

At times, we are inspired by the senses that we lack. Helen Keller could not see or hear, but she relied on the senses she could use to see a different perspective than most, using her knowledge to share her heart with the world. The loss of one sense has driven many people to write, sometimes resulting in success as an author.

Some writers also like to explore the sixth sense, which may be viewed as perspective, insight, or vision. For some, it is the gut instinct. For others it is a peek into the unknown future.

Our Experiences

We have all experienced love and loss, major events, relationships, adventure. Those experiences shape us and inspire us to write. Children rely on personal experience to keep a journal, the first foray into writing for many authors. Some common threads in these early journals include these questions:

- How do we develop friendship?
- How do we break up with a former flame?
- Did an event such as a costume party or holiday leave a lasting impression?
- Where is a favorite place to vacation?
- Was one year of school especially awkward? Why?

The more we study and learn, the more we interact with the world around us, the more hobbies we have, the more "first" experiences we make for ourselves, the more people we meet and converse with, the more experiences we have to draw upon.

Feelings and Emotions

This is closely related to our experiences, but focuses on the internal way in which we respond to our five senses and our experiences.

- What does it feel like to fall in love?

- How does it feel to lie or be lied to?

- What do we do when faced with a new situation?

- What does regret feel like?

- What does bliss feel like?

- How are day-to-day emotions different from the emotions of a single event, such as a wedding, the birth of a child, or the death of a loved one?

To immerse ourselves in emotion, we must take a moment to turn off the organizer—the thinker, the inner editor—and go with the flow of feelings.

When looking for story inspiration, it is good to examine these three sources. Ultimately, the best story may be inspired by one, but reflect all three.

Exercise Five: Shopping for Story Ideas

Now that we've discussed how stories are generated—through our senses, experiences, and emotions, surely you are ready to sit down and write your story.

Not quite?

The next exercise is designed to help you train your brain to generate story ideas, even when you have very little time, inspiration, or opportunity to write.

During the Writing Day workshop, we discussed the aforementioned sources for story inspiration, but knew that in the spirit of the moment, it was unlikely a mere discussion about those sources would suffice. The writers featured in this anthology would need a little extra dose of inspiration to create a story ripe for publication (in a single afternoon), so to assist in idea generation, we used a technique called "Shopping for Story Ideas."

We provided three boxes of inspirational materials. In the first were photographs of stores from around the world. In the second were different character types, and in the third were conflicts. Writers started with two photos, then reached into the conflicts and characters boxes for additional inspiration as needed.

To prepare for this exercise, you will need:

*Photos of stores** (included in this book)

*Character types (included in this book)

*Conflicts (included in this book)

*Laptop or pen(cil) and paper

*Timer

**If you are doing this exercise at home or with internet access, you may google "shop" or "store" for additional images. This book contains several photos from MorgueFile, a free photo sharing site for creative types.

The Rules:

- Set a timer for 15 minutes.

- Pick one to two photos from the options provided.

- Spend a few seconds looking at the photo(s).

- Brainstorm story ideas.

- If a brainstorm does not come, proceed with character types and conflicts, and then put your character and/or conflict into the store setting from your photo.

- Jot down your story ideas.

Tips:

- If you are not inspired by a photo, character, or conflict, change. But change quickly so you don't run out of time.

- Do not edit your brainstorm. Allow the ideas to flow, no matter how weak or strong they resonate in your mind.

- This is not the time to write a story. Limit your ideas to one to two sentences. The story will come later.

- Try not to follow any one train of thought for too long. The idea here is to generate a lot of ideas, much like the free writing exercise.

- Since it would take you more than 15 minutes to browse all the photos and read through the character and conflict lists, you may want to close your eyes and point to one to two items on each list. Once you have finished the exercise, feel free to go back and read through the lists.

Exercise 5A: Photos

Thank you to the Morgue File contributors for the following photos of international shops.

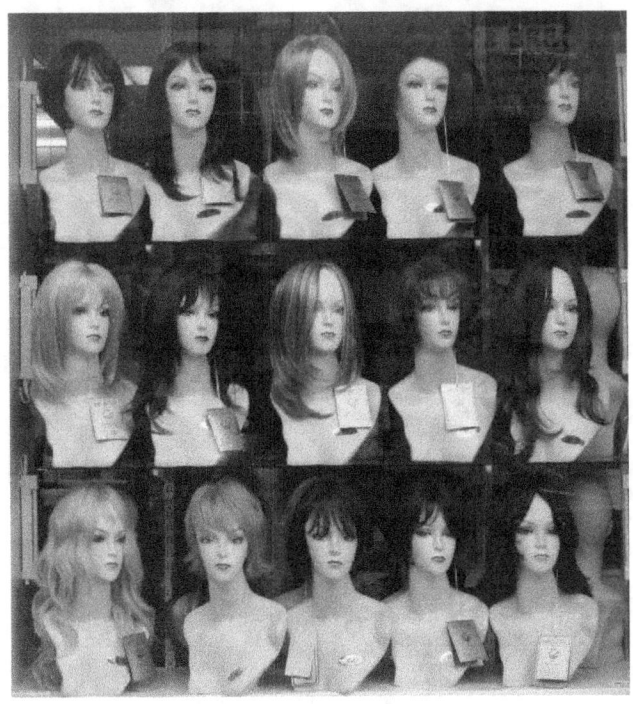

Exercise 5B: Character Types

If you are ready to brainstorm story ideas from the photo selected, great! Start compiling your list of ideas! If you still need a little inspiration, read on.

Writing day workshop participants were invited to welcome inspiration from a wide variety of character archetypes. Each archetype had positive and negative associations for that type of character. For example, an engineer may be characterized as one who can solve problems and work in innovative ways, but also seen as rigid and lacking emotion. A clergyman may be characterized as selfless, dignified, and charitable, but also lonely and distant from the society or with a tendency to live on a pedestal. A mother may be characterized as a warm and nurturing guide, but also blind to her offspring's defects.

None of the characterizations are fully true—they are based on assumptions and prejudice—but since it is likely that your character will live in a world where assumption and prejudice exist, it is useful to know how your character may be viewed by others. From there, you may choose to play up how your character differs from assumed traits or how they fall into societal expectations and norms.

Types may be defined by a character's role in society, their job, family status, age, or traits. Character types may be real, as with a mother or a school principal, or imagined, as with a fairy or a zombie.

In this book, we provide you with the character type, but leave the positive and negative associations to you. The lists are far from exhaustive, but should serve you with a jumping-off point. The character types below are grouped by role in society, but listed in no particular order.

Familial Roles

- Mother
- Father
- Child
- Sister
- Brother
- Stepchild
- Stepparent
- Grandmother
- Grandfather
- Godparent
- Aunt
- Uncle
- Cousin
- Niece
- Nephew
- Orphan
- Foster Parent
- Pet

Careers

- President
- King
- Queen
- Teacher (Preschool? Middle School? College?)
- Custodian
- Store Manager
- Hairdresser
- Editor
- Writer
- Painter
- Sculptor
- Clergy: Minister, Priest, Nun
- Addictions Counselor
- School Counselor
- Camp Counselor
- Engineer
- Doctor
- Librarian
- Social Worker
- Nurse
- Builder
- Architect
- CEO
- Banker

- Lawyer
- Mayor
- Police Officer
- Fireman/woman
- Postman/woman
- Poet
- Fortune Teller
- Maid
- Homemaker
- Chef
- Actor
- Singer
- Musician
- Athlete
- Student

Personalities and Character Traits

- Bully
- Lover
- Friend
- Mentor
- Visionary
- Naive
- Wise
- Leader

- Follower
- Forgiving
- Jealous
- Agreeable
- Discontent
- Conscientious
- Selfish
- Angry
- Self-assured
- Doubtful
- Narcissistic
- Warm

Magic

- Witch
- Wizard
- Fairy
- Zombie
- Eternal Life
- Shape Shifter
- Time Traveler
- Vampire
- God
- Goddess
- Werewolf

Exercise 5C: Conflict

Stories cannot move forward and characters cannot grow without conflict. And without conflict, readers will lose interest.

Workshop attendees were allowed to pick one or two of the following conflicts from a box. Again, do not read through the list. Close your eyes and point to one or two conflicts and then revisit this list as needed in your writing. Find a way to work your chosen conflict into the store scene.

Warning: if you are writing for children, especially young children in the picture book through early reader phases, several of the conflicts on this list will not fit with your genre. Focus on conflicts children go through—moving; making friends; losing friends, pets, or grandparents; bullies; feeling misunderstood or confused. However, most conflicts on the following list will be appropriate for young adult literature, and several will fit middle grade.

Conflicts

- Serious illness
- Troublesome street gang
- Torn between two things
- Air raid
- Hurricane
- Serious wound
- Ticking clock
- Earthquake
- Pollution

- Tsunami
- Wildfire
- Technology problems
- Dark brotherhood
- Trickster
- Drug pusher
- Plague
- Dangerous animal
- Evil corporation
- Temptress
- Evil Stepmom
- Deadbeat Dad
- Pirates
- Traitors
- Dictator
- Cult leader
- Evil twins
- Rebels
- Bad cop
- Tyrant
- Mad scientist
- Psychopath
- Pedophile
- Racism
- Cultural clashes

- Vikings

- Serial killer

- Bad stereotype

- Sexism

- Vandals

- Mafia / Organized crime

- Misguided religious leader

- Bureaucracy

- Evil empire

- Evil witch

- Witch hunt

- Secret society

- War

- Possessed shaman

- Dark wizard

- Destructive gods / goddesses

- Angry ghost

- Zombies

- Monsters

- Haunted house

- Internal conflict: shame

- Thirsty vampire

- Werewolf on the loose

- Unfriendly space aliens

- Internal conflict: guilt

- Internal conflict: grief
- Internal conflict: anger
- Internal conflict: bad luck
- Internal conflict: karma
- Curses
- Nuclear disaster
- Thief
- Bridge collapse
- Railroad accident
- Car accident
- Terrorists
- Plane crash
- Massacre
- Rogue cop
- Radioactive fallout
- Widespread power outage
- Riots
- Murder
- Shipwreck
- Flood
- Industrial accident
- Volcanic eruption
- Avalanche
- Drought
- Bomb

- Divorce
- Blizzard
- Heat wave
- Epidemic
- Building collapse
- Martial law

Exercise Six: Sharing Ideas

This exercise is optimized for a workshop or classroom experience, but it is no less important in a writer's life. Since ideas are born of other ideas, and an open forum and exchange to discuss ideas offer a different perspective, workshop attendees were encouraged to share their story ideas.

Fifteen minutes were set aside for discussion, and Writing Day participants engaged in a round table as they held up the photo selected and shared the story idea inspired by the photo.

If you are following along at home, you may wish to set a date to meet with writing friends and share ideas with one another. We often meet with other writers to critique the craft once the story has been set in an effort to strengthen revisions, but sometimes it is valuable to toss ideas back and forth before we arrive at the point of writing the story. If you run a blog or engage in social media with writers, feel free to share a concept and get feedback. Play a game of "what if?" with friends and family to generate new story ideas.

Exercise Seven: Putting Your Story Ideas to Use

Next, it is time to move from story idea to first draft.

For this exercise, you will need:

*Photo

*Laptop or pen(cil) and paper

*Timer

*Character prompt (if applicable)

*Conflict prompt (if applicable)

Look through the story ideas you created in the "Shopping for Story Ideas" exercise and circle the one you are most drawn towards. You may find you like elements of a couple of ideas combined or that the process of sharing ideas with other writers resulted in a "light bulb" moment of clarity. Highlight, circle, underline, or make red marks on your most promising ideas. Now it is time to get to work.

The Rules:

- Set a timer for 45 minutes.

- Pick your favorite story idea(s) from exercises five and six.

- Choose the genre you'd like for your piece: poetry, picture book, flash fiction, or essay. (Use the guideline, tips, and techniques in the appendix for the four literary forms recommended. These four literary forms were selected for their brevity and potential to pack a punch in short form.)

- Write.

If you need additional inspiration, flip back to the character types and conflicts. Think about the five senses as well as the feelings and emotions your characters may be experiencing. Ask yourself two questions along the way—"what if?" and "why?"

Refining Your Piece

Everything you write has to be revised, whether you have given yourself 45 minutes or four years to hammer out your first draft. The first draft is like a pre-game practice run—great for warming up and getting a few technical drills underway, but ultimately untested.

In order to give the CBW-LA Writing Day workshop attendees the best opportunity for a solid anthology piece, we conducted two revision exercises.

Exercise Eight: Point of View

Our first revision exercise focused on the point of view. Time for another refresher?

There are three points of view: first person, second person, and third person. The difference between points of view may appear slight, grammatically speaking, but a change in point of view has the power to alter the tone of a piece. It also allows the author and the narrator the ability to change perspective.

First person stories are written using the pronouns I and we. Young adult novels are often written in the first person because the protagonist becomes the narrator; it gives the author an opportunity to delve deep into emotions, thoughts, and psychological nuance. In the first person, hopes and dreams, fears and doubts, and imagination become paramount.

Second person stories are written using the pronoun you. The second person is rarely used in narrative literature, such as prose, but it is seen in poetry, particularly in odes. In second person, the narrator focuses outward on his or her perception of another character. Second person would be used more often in marketing material, such as advertisements or slogans, but it can be a useful point of view for a revision exercise to come to a deeper understanding of your material. For example, if you write a young adult novel in the first person, it may help you understand how the world sees the character if you do a brief rewrite of the second person, in which another character central your your protagonist's life writes to him or her. It may even guide you towards a new take on the relationship between the protagonist and the supporting character, whether that is a sibling, parent, friend or significant other.

Third person stories are written using the pronouns he, she, and they. The third person is very common in picture books and flash fiction, with an omniscient narrator who recounts the story of all the characters, generally focused on one or a few, but with the advantage of omnipresence.

In order to complete exercise seven, you subconsciously chose one point of view. Chances are that with the time crunch, you traveled into your comfort zone or instinctually felt that one point of view would work better than another with your story idea.

Now it is time to flip things around a little bit and make sure your story or poem is being recounted by the right person.

To complete this exercise, you will need:

*Original piece from exercise seven

*Laptop or pen(cil) and paper

*Timer

The Rules:

- Set the timer for 15 minutes.
- Identify your original point of view.
- Pick an alternate point of view for your piece.
- Rewrite your story.

This will not be a perfect revision. The 15 minute time limit is just enough to allow you to explore whether another point of view will work better. You may also learn something new about your character or story by changing your narrator.

Exercise Eight Wrap-Up:

- Read both your original story and the new point of view.
- Determine which point of view works best for your piece.
- Use this point of view for the next exercise.

Exercise Nine: Tone Twist and Voice

What is voice in a story? How does it differ from point of view or character?

Voice is one of those slippery concepts that is difficult to define but evident when done correctly—and equally evident when missing the mark.

Voice is the quality of the narration, regardless of whether the story is told in the first, second, or third person. Is the voice casual and friendly (like this book)? Is it stark and professional? Maybe it's dark and scary? The voice is essentially the personality of the book. That does not necessarily mean it is the personality of the narrator.

Tone differs from voice in that tone is the atmosphere of the book. The tone may be threatening, as in a thriller, or light and airy, as in a chick lit book. Tone and voice do not have to match, and if done well, a disconnect between voice and tone may bring depth to a project or reveal idiosyncrasies. Satires are good examples of dissonant tone and voice. In general, though, it is a good idea to have a tone and voice working in partnership.

Your selected voice will determine the mood of the entire story. Is your voice ironic? Comic? Detached? Serious? Entertaining? Light-hearted? Sad?

This exercise will allow you to play a little with both voice and tone as you tap into the emotion of the piece.

To complete this exercise, you will need:

*Original piece from exercise seven

*Laptop or pen(cil) and paper

*Timer

The Rules:

- Set the timer for 15 minutes.

- Identify your narrator, using the point of view from exercise eight.

- Rewrite your piece using a different tone, in a voice that compliments that tone. For example, rewrite your piece as if everything in the story infuriated you. Or broke your heart. Or scared the bejeezus out of you. Or put you in a state of confusion. Or tickled your funny bone. This exercise challenges you to tap into different emotions.

Once time is up, identify which voice felt more natural to you and which one lends itself best to the story you are telling.

Tips:

- The voice you choose will either belong to a removed narrator or to a character in the book. Identify who owns your voice.

- Pay attention to common voices in different genres. Fantasy and historical fiction are often told through a formal voice, peppered with old-fashioned words and phrases to transport the reader to a different mindset, place, or time. Comic and chick lit stories are generally told in a light, casual voice.

- Every author carries with him or her a natural voice, a unique thumbprint to his or her work. Beyond that, each story demands its own narrator's voice to complement the tale. Whether a story is told in the first or third person, the voice must be tailor-made for the story and subject.

- Rather than attempt to make your narrator disappear, think of your narrative voice as another character in your book.

- Remember that the voice you use will influence how your reader feels about the story.

- Consistency of voice is critical. You might be ironic one minute and innocent the next, but the reader should be able to depend on your narrative voice to remain essentially the same throughout the book.

- Some authors choose to weave multiple characters and voices into a storyline, such as the middle grade novel Wonder by R.J. Palacio. If you are writing a story with multiple voices, take time to read each character's contribution, on its own, in linear form. Make sure each character owns a singular voice that remains consistent throughout the story. Then take time to read the characters' voices side-by-side. See if each voice sounds different and recognizable (without character subtitles for identification). Writing in multiple voices is very challenging and best left for longer literary styles.

- For the exercises in this book, we recommend focusing on one voice at a time.

Exercise Ten: Polish and Shine

You've come a long way. You've generated a story idea, written a first draft, and completed two revisions. Give yourself a pat on the back and go grab another round of tea or coffee. We've arrived at the last exercise.

In this exercise, you will combine the insight and techniques you've learned through revision to refine your story into its final form.

Here's what you will need:

*Original piece, point of view revision, voice revision

*Laptop or pen(cil) and paper

*Timer

The Rules:

- Set the timer for one hour.

- Read through and review all three pieces.

- Weave your best work together, taking into account the best point of view and voice you identified in your revision exercises.

- Check for grammar.

- Check for consistency in voice.

- Make sure your story has a beginning, middle, and end, sprinkled with conflict and compelling characters.

- Polish, shine, perfect.

- Use the appendix on the four literary forms as a guide when stuck.

Once the timer dings, take in a deep breath of satisfaction and walk away from your piece.

If you are following along at home, you have now completed a first draft, with three revisions between exercises five through ten, in less than half a day. Congratulations! Now set your work aside and come back to it next week to see if you might like to continue working on your story.

Turn the page to see what the aspiring and published authors at the CBW-LA Writing Day Workshop composed in one day…without second chances!

Section 4

Anthology Pieces

Essay

Story Gardener

By Nutschell Anne Windsor

I planted a seed of ideas in the ground, buried it under the rich soil of labor, watered it with sweat and tears, and waited for it to blossom.

In my mind, I beheld a majestic tree, its roots reaching long and deep into the hearts of its listeners, its branches reaching up to the sky of everyone's minds. Its leaves were pages that rode with the wind to other lands, catching fire to warm a little girl's lonely ache or dissolving like fertilizer to make a little boy's curiosity grow.

I tended this seed every day until it grew into a sapling. The sight of its tiny leaves gave me hope, and I envisioned its branches heavy with the weight of a million golden fruits. I could already taste the sweet fruits it would bear, could see the many people these fruits would nourish.

Years passed, and the sapling grew into a tree. It wasn't as grand as I had imagined it would be. Its roots were weak, its branches thin, and its leaves were few. I pruned the wayward limbs, trimmed the yellowing foliage, and even replanted it in a bigger pot to give it room to grow.

But no matter what I did, the tree did not bear fruit. Until one day a storm arrived, vicious and relentless. It left behind a trail of soggy leaves and broken branches; the beautiful tree I had tended for years died in the span of one night.

I wept for the majestic tree I would never see, for the sweet fruit I would never taste. And I vowed I would give up gardening words completely.

But the blank canvas of the earth called to me and the sun shone bright, showing me the beauty of what might still be.

And so I began again.

I chose another idea seed from my mind's jar and planted it in the ground.

After a year, it has already grown into a new sapling.

I tend to it every day, infusing the soil with the nutrient of books and showering it with the waters of encouragement. With shears of constructive criticism, I prune the limbs of my beloved story tree, and, with a steady trowel in my hands, I mercilessly cut down the weeds of unnecessary words.

The vision of the golden fruits still lures me with its promises, but they are not what drive me now. I love hunting for new seeds to plant and the feel of the earth beneath my fingers. I love the pain that comes with digging, and weeding, and pruning.

I know that no matter how many storms I need to weather, how many seeds I may waste, how many saplings I may have to watch die, I will continue to do this every day. Because I am a gardener of words, and though the fruits may bring promises of happiness, it is the labor that I truly enjoy.

Picture Book

The Magic Pinwheel

By Tiffani Barth

Autumn leaves fell on my head as I sat on the front steps and watched my friends ride past me on their brand new bikes. They whizzed back and forth through the fog, their hoots of laughter echoing off the nearby apartment buildings.

"Come on, Sam," they called, ringing their bells and honking their horns.

It sounded much too loud in the otherwise silent neighborhood. I shook my head, feeling the damp chill sink even deeper into my skin.

"Sam's such a baby," said Max, a tall boy who sat two desks away from me in class. "He doesn't even know how to ride a bike."

"Yes I do," I said, feeling my lip tremble. It was true. I knew how to ride—I just couldn't do it.

"Prove it," said Max. He got off his bike and motioned for me to come over.

With stiff limbs, I approached the bike and got on. The seat was way too high for me. Why hadn't I just 'fessed up? Now I was really gonna get it. The other boys all moved aside to give me room. I lifted my feet off the ground and began to pedal. The bike wobbled. I pumped the pedals up and down and then felt myself leaning too far to one side. The bike tipped, sending me crashing to the pavement.

I cried out in pain as Max laughed and pointed at me. He picked up the bike while I rubbed a sore knee. "Look, now the baby's crying."

Some of the other kids covered their mouths, but I knew that they were laughing at me.

I stood up and limped back to my house as the other kids rode away. Grandpa greeted me at the door and helped me inside. I sat in a chair while he fetched an icepack for my knee. It was turning purple.

"You should try my pinwheel," he said, examining the injury.

"Your pinwheel?"

Grandpa smiled. "It's for stability." Grandpa went upstairs and came back carrying a shiny pinwheel. It was small and multicolored, with a pink flower in the middle.

I wrinkled my nose. *How could that thing help me ride?* "Those are for girls," I said. "Max will make fun of me even more."

"Give it a try," said Grandpa. "You might be surprised." He set the pinwheel on the table and left the room.

I stared at the little pinwheel for a long time. I thought about Max and the other kids our age. It seemed like everyone else I knew could ride a bike. Why was it so hard for me?

Well, I certainly didn't need some girly pinwheel to help me.

I went out into the garage and rolled my bike out into the driveway. I could do it this time, I knew I could. With shaking hands I gripped the handlebars and then quickly raised my feet to the pedals. The bike began to roll forward. I started to pedal faster. The bike zipped ahead. I tried to keep pedaling but suddenly lost control. The bike crashed into the curb, sending me tumbling to the ground.

I kicked my bike and crossed my arms. I could feel the tears coming, but I refused to let them fall. Sniffling, I went back inside. The colorful pinwheel once again caught my eye.

With a big sigh, I picked it up and blew on it, watching the colors swirl around and around. As long as no one was looking, it couldn't hurt to try it.

I brought the pinwheel outside and fastened it between the handlebars of my bike with some old shoelaces. Bravely, I mounted my bike, feeling a surge of confidence race through me. As I began to pedal, the pinwheel turned around and around so fast I couldn't even see the pink flower on the front. It made a puttering sound like a little motor.

The bike rolled forward, and I sped down the street. I was doing it. I was riding! A big smile spread across my face as I pedaled faster and faster. The wind rushed past my face and through my hair, making it feel like I was flying. Looking down, I realized it wasn't just a feeling. I was flying!

I peered at the houses and streets in my neighborhood. I flew above the fog, over rooftops and swimming pools, over yards and around tall trees. Suddenly, I spotted Max and his other friends riding their bikes a couple streets down. I flew a little lower and raced past them, yelling and laughing with exhilaration.

Max looked up, his eyes very wide. "H-how are you doing that?"

"It's my pinwheel," I called back, even as I rose higher. "It's magic."

Finally it was time to go home. I touched down in my driveway and got off my bike. As I was rolling it back to the garage, I looked up to see Grandpa looking at me from the window. There was a knowing smile on his face.

The next day as I went outside to get the mail, I saw Max ride by. There was a little pinwheel tied to his handlebars. Max was pedaling so fast that he was out of breath and sweat was pouring down his face, but he was still on the ground.

I just smiled to myself.

"Max is such a baby. He doesn't even know how to fly."

Sweet Tooth Aliens

By Abi Estrin

Boom! Crash! Zing!

The aliens landed in the middle of the night.

Mrs. Greggors was snoring.

Mr. Jenson was watching late-night TV.

Old Martha McMuffins was dreaming of her candy shop, filled with chocolates, saltwater taffy, and peppermint cream bars.

Sarah was sound asleep in her cozy bed, her cat Ginger curled up on her head.

"Mech, mech!"

"Zebb, zebb!"

The aliens oozed out of their metal ship.

Out they came, three tentacles each.

Two eyes for a nose.

Two noses for an ear.

They were hideous looking things...

And they were HUNGRY.

They slithered into town, looking for food...

Human food...

"Meeeow!!!" Ginger jumped out of bed.

Sarah leapt up with a start.

"Am I dreaming?" cried Sarah, peering out her bedroom window at dozens of glowing alien tentacles. She pinched herself, but they were real.

Sarah grabbed her sneakers and jacket. "Wake up!" she shouted. "Everybody wake up!"

"Huh?" grumbled Mr. Greggors.

"Eh?" said Mr. Jenson.

"Who?" shouted old Martha McMuffins.

"ALIENS!" hollered Sarah.

The sirens went off. Whhhirrrr!

Everybody was awake. All the townspeople ran into Main Street in their pajamas and robes and fuzzy slippers and hair curlers.

"Mech, mech!" said the aliens.

"Zebb, zebb!"

They trampled on the tomato garden and overturned garbage cans.

They oozed into the street, sending their tentacles in every direction.

They even went into the pizza parlor and threw breadsticks and marinara sauce everywhere, creating such a mess!

"Ginger," Sarah whispered as they oozed over the playground, "I think these are bad aliens...."

Ginger's hair stood on end, and he growled in agreement.

Old Martha McMuffins screamed, "Oh no! My candy shop!" And then she fainted.

All the aliens oozed through the door. The entire candy shop was filled with a green light. The aliens started sucking up all the chocolates and gummies and peppermint candy canes from McMuffin's Candy Company.

Ginger ran into the candy shop and started hissing and spitting and growling at the aliens.

"No, Ginger!" shouted Sarah.

"Mech, mech, MECH!!!" said the aliens.
"Zeb, zeb, candy!!!!"

"They want CANDY!" Sarah exclaimed.

"Hands off our candy shop!!!" shouted Mrs. Greggor.

"Stay away from the cream puffs!" shouted Mr. Jensen.

Martha McMuffins regained consciousness for a moment, just long enough to stay, "Keep your hands off my chocolates!"

Just then, the aliens oozed up to where Ginger was crouching, overturning a case of peanut brittle.

"ENOUGH!" shouted Sarah, running in to scoop Ginger up in her arms. Then Sarah bravely ripped a candy cane out of one of the alien's mouths.

"Mech....?"

"Where are your manners, aliens?"

The aliens raised their tentacles, listening...

"On Earth," Sarah continued, "everybody learns to share. And just look at the mess you've created!"

"You even made Martha McMuffins faint! This is her candy shop, you know!"

The aliens shook their oozing tentacles and drooped in embarrassment.

"Mech, mech..." they muttered.

"Zebb, zebb...we're sorry," they said. "We ran out of candy on our planet. We didn't know what to do!"

"It's okay," Sarah said, patting one of their green tentacles. "Let's clean up together and then we'll share our candy. And if you're nice to Martha McMuffins, maybe she'll even make you more candy for your trip back to your home planet."

Everybody clapped.

The aliens wiggled with joy.

Ginger purred.

The aliens used their space lasers to put everything back where it belonged, cleaning up all their mess, and they even helped Martha McMuffins bake brand-new green candy just for the shop.

"Bye!" waved Sarah.

"Mech, mech!" said the aliens.

Everybody waved goodbye.

"Zebb! Zebb! Zebb!"

For Want of a Better Thing

By Glenn Jason Hanna

"What can I do you for?" Penelope asked the little boy who came into her store.

"I need to buy some wants," Kevin said.

"You're in luck," the young woman said. "I'm running a special this week—three wants for a penny. What wants would you like?"

Kevin thought of the things he hated to do most of all.

"I want to like vegetables, I want to like homework, and I want to like playing with my gross cousin, Susie."

Penelope gave Kevin his wants, he gave her a penny, and whistling down the street walked a very happy boy.

Normally at dinner, Kevin would eat the meat first—beef, pork or chicken. Then the starch next—usually rice or potatoes of some kind. Then he would hold his nose while he forced the vile vegetables down his unwilling throat.

But not this time. He wolfed the Brussels sprouts down as fast as he could.

After dinner, Kevin sat down to do his homework. Normally he would spin in his chair, surf the internet, and throw pencils into the ceiling before hurrying through his homework, doing well enough to pass with a 'C' on most days. But not this time.

This time, Kevin joyfully, thoroughly completed his work. Then he did the next night's homework. And the next. And the next, and all the extra credit, too.

The next day was Saturday, and Kevin's cousin, Susie, came over. Normally, Kevin would pull her braids, hide her shoes, and flush her inhaler down the toilet.

But not this time. He offered to play anything Susie wanted, even if it meant playing house. And he didn't complain a bit, even when she made him wear the blue dress.

So it continued for weeks on end. Kevin ate his vegetables, did his homework and played nicely with Susie.

Penelope was surprised when Kevin glumly marched into her store.

"What's the matter, young man?" she asked. "Didn't my wants serve you well?"

"Yeah, they worked. Too well. That's the problem. All I eat are vegetables, and now I have an iron deficiency. I do so much homework, I don't do anything else, and my other friends dumped me because all I do is play with Susie."

"So you want to return the wants?"

"Heck no, I want some more," Kevin said, holding up a penny. "I want to like other foods as much as vegetables, I want to like to play as much as doing homework, and I want to like other people as much as Susie."

So Penelope gave Kevin his wants, and he gave her a penny, and whistling down the street walked a very happy boy.

After gulping down the three new vials of wants Penelope gave him, Kevin sat down to dinner. He ate his vegetables just as before. He also ate the chicken, the rice, the dog, his napkin, his shirt. He even bit his own hand once or twice.

When he sat down to do his homework, he worked for an hour before taking a break to play the *Knights of Death* video game. Then he did another hour of homework before taking a break to complete two 250-piece puzzles. Kevin alternated between homework and funwork until the wee hours of the morning.

When Susie came over, he played nicely with her, but he wasn't happy when she left to go home. So Kevin went to play with Richard down the block, Wayne across the street, and Tucker one street over. He played with the older kids in the park, the younger kids in the sand box. Even that kid who thinks he's a princess and his dog's a magical horse.

And so it continued for weeks on end. Kevin ate everything, did everything, played nicely with everyone.

Again, Penelope was surprised when Kevin glumly marched into her store.

"What's the matter, young man?" she asked. "Didn't my wants serve you well?"

"Yeah, they did. That's the problem. I eat so much that I gained 50 pounds. I do so much that I'm tired all the time. And people flee when they see me because they're sick of playing with me."

"So you want to return the wants?"

"Heck no, I want a want to undo the wants I wanted before," Kevin said, holding up a penny.

"You want to want nothing?"

"Yes, that's what I want."

So Penelope gave Kevin his want, and he gave her a penny, and whistling down the street walked a very happy boy.

But when Kevin sat down to dinner, he ate nothing at all. When it was time for homework, he did nothing at all. When Susie or anyone else came over, he ignored them. Kevin did nothing but sit in the corner, in the dark, for weeks on end, doing absolutely nothing.

This time Penelope was not surprised when Kevin dragged his lethargic body into her store.

"This sucks," Kevin said. "If I want some things, then I do them and nothing else and that's not good. If I want everything, I do too much and that's not good. If I want nothing, I sit in the corner all day staring into space and that's not good. What I am supposed to want and not want?"

"You want to know?" Penelope said.

"Yeah, I do," Kevin said.

"Then here. Free of charge."

Penelope held out another small vial for Kevin.

But Kevin didn't want it or any of the other wants he bought. He put all of the vials on the counter.

"Keep them and keep my money, too" he said. "I just want to go home."

So home he went.

The next time Kevin sat down to dinner, he ate his steak first, his potatoes second and then the Brussels sprouts. He still didn't like them, but they weren't so bad.

When he sat down to do his homework, he did his best before playing the *Knights of Death*.

When Susie came over to play, Kevin made her a deal. First they played a game he wanted for an hour. Then they played a game she wanted for an hour. Kevin still didn't like playing house, but he realized it wasn't so bad. So long as he didn't have to put on the blue dress.

And so Kevin lived his life, doing the things he liked to do and doing the best he could with the things that he had to do, but didn't like so much. After all, what else could he really do?

The Girl Who Revealed the Creature

By Cameron Ulyate

Amy squeezed her wrench as she crept through the run-down castle. *There they are,* she thought. Her journey had been long. After spending the last five hours traveling through a dangerous mechanical forest, she thought she might never find the blueprints. But now she saw them, sitting on an old table.

"Ok Amy, all you have to do is grab the inventor's blueprints, run back to Steamville, and build something before the mayor forecloses the house," she whispered to herself. "You need to make Papa proud."

A huge door burst open, and a giant creature, eight feet tall with mechanical armor, jumped in front of the blueprints. The creature stared at Amy with its glowing red eyes. It breathed heavily as steam flowed out from the pipes in its back.

Amy stuttered. "It is okay...I just...want the blueprints. I know you're the inventor's pet. Please, I need them."

The creature walked toward Amy until it was face to face with her. The creature growled like the sound of two pipes smashing together.

Amy bolted, running around the room, the creature right behind her, smacking everything out of control. It reached out to catch her. Amy dashed behind a wall, and the creature's hand broke as it hit the wall.

Amy heard what sounded like cries. She stepped out from behind the wall. The creature's red eyes turned to blue as it panicked and tried to put the broken hand back on. The hand fell off again and the creature screamed.

Amy took her chance and grabbed the blueprints.

"These are instructions on how the creature was made," she told herself.

Amy heard a faint voice come from the creature and looked up at him.

"Please, I'm not the inventor's pet. My dad built the armor to keep me alive. Without it I will die."

Amy walked over to the creature and took the broken hand. She grabbed her wrench and screwed the hand back onto the creature. She read the blueprints.

"Wait, this part that looks like a heart is preserving you, not the armor," Amy said.

Amy pulled off the helmet and the armor started to fall apart. Inside the armor was a young boy the same age as Amy. The boy jumped.

"What are you doing?" he yelled, as he began to breathe heavily.

"You're fine. See, this is what's keeping you alive."

Amy pointed to the mechanical blue heart breathing rapidly with wires connected to the boy's chest.

"All along, the creature that guarded the great inventor's blueprints was actually just you trying to stay alive. I feel like the bad guy now," Amy huffed. "I just needed a few inventions to sell to the mayor so my father and I could stay in our home."

"Wait, my father has a lot of unfinished inventions upstairs. I'll let you have them, if you let me come with you. This castle gets very lonely."

Amy smiled. *Yes, I'll be able to save my home.*

"Alright. We better get to work. Then you can have some of Papa's delicious soup."

Wishing Hair

By Alana Garrigues

Twinkle! Sparkle! Sprinkle! Shine!

Betsy looked up, curious whether her mom had seen the magic. She knew that grown-ups didn't usually see special things like fairies and sparkle dust. Always rushing here and there, looking ahead, worrying about this and that. Kids were much better at noticing the magic.

Grown-ups like to call magic childish words like "imaginary" or "make-believe," always trying to use science or reason to explain things.

But kids know the truth. Kids understand fairies and leprechauns and wishes on a dandelion and just how important it is to blow out all the candles on a birthday cake.

As Betsy raised her head, she caught her mom's reflection first in the wig shop windowpane. Mom was standing still, mouth agape, a flickering in her eyes.

"Mom, did you see it? Did you see the sparkle?"

"I did! It's leaping and dancing in the window. What is that?"

It looked like rainbows dancing from a crystal ball, but there was no sun amid the flurries of snow. Something else was happening in the store.

"It's magic, Mom!"

"Magic? I don't know about that, Betsy, but we have a little time. Do you want to go in and see what it's all about?"

A grown-up offering to dilly-dally and explore the magic? Do ducks waddle? Of course Betsy wanted to go inside.

As mom and daughter entered the store, they noticed every wig swished in the breeze.

"Welcome," the woman at the register beamed. "Please, do come in. Take a look around."

"Your wigs, they're … lovely. So sparkly," Betsy's mom said.

The storeowner smiled and bowed her head.

"Thank you," she said. "These are magical wigs. I think you'll be very pleased with our selection. Please, let me know if you have any questions."

Betsy thought the woman looked so familiar with her big, blue eyes, long, blonde hair, warm, welcoming smile, and out-of-the-ordinary bare feet. All at once, she realized it was Rapunzel!

"Princess, what are you doing here?" Betsy asked.

"After I left the tower, my hair continued to grow. It was of no use to me anymore. I had no one to lift with my long tresses, and it kept getting tangled and in the way. So I decided to cut it. And it grew back. So I cut it again, and it grew back again. And again. And again.

"One day, my niece Marla put some of my old hair on her head to play make-believe princess. During their game, she made a wish to sleep in a bed of flowers.

"When she went back home that night, Marla opened her bedroom door. Instead of her bed, she saw a hammock of daisies and tulips suspended in air!

"From then on, anytime she put the hair on her head, she made a wish. She wished for cotton candy, a new puppy, a day without chores, an automatic hair brusher, a hot air balloon ride, and a best friend.

"The moment she made a wish, as long as she was wearing the hair, her wish came true," said Rapunzel. "So I decided to share my wishing hair with all the little girls in the kingdom. I opened this shop two days ago."

"Will it really work, Princess Rapunzel? Even on a normal girl like me?"

"Do you believe in magic?"

"Yes! I do. I believe in magic with all of my heart."

"Then it will really work."

Betsy's mom looked doubtful, but who was she to disagree with a princess? She let Betsy choose an auburn wig and they walked out of the store.

The minute they left, Betsy put the wig on and began making wishes.

"A kitten! A baby brother! A new bike! A castle for my family! Sunshine! Dinner with the tooth fairy! An airplane! A trip to the moon!"

Every wish came true. The bigger Betsy wished, the more elaborate her family's life became. She was surrounded by extravagant food and gifts and lots of friends.

But Betsy wasn't happy. All this wishing for things kept her very busy. And she noticed all of her friends started their conversations with, "Let's wish for ..."

Sometimes, she thought they just wanted to be her friend to get new stuff.

Plus, she couldn't play make-believe games with her friends anymore because everything they said would come true.

One time, Betsy and her best friend Lucy imagined a tea party with an elephant and a lion. All of a sudden, a huge gray guest and his trusty regal sidekick showed up with tea and crumpets.

It was all just too much.

Betsy started to "lose" the wig on purpose and invite her friends to play without all the wishing. But once they figured out they couldn't get anything new, they would go home.

Betsy went back to the store.

"Hello, Betsy. Welcome back! How is my hair treating you?" asked Rapunzel.

"Not so well, Princess. I already wished for so many things that I am running out of ideas. My house is a mess. I'm always busy trying to keep track of my stuff. Plus, I can't tell who my real friends are and who is just faking," said Betsy.

"Ah, yes, that is a problem. I remember the feeling well. Hmm, I'd say we have two options—return the wig, and with it all of the magic that the wig has granted you, or sign up for my class in wig control and learn to be the boss of your wig instead of letting it be the boss of you."

"Wig control? Sign me up," said Betsy, not really wanting to give up her family's castle for a returned wig.

From that day forward, Betsy met with the princess every day after school to talk about hard work, friendship, and earned rewards. She learned to set the wig aside and only pull it out for very special occasions such as slumber parties or to celebrate excellent test scores. Best of all, she and her friends got back to giggling and make-believe "like all little girls should." (At least that's what grown-ups said.)

Betsy just knew giggling and make-believe made her even happier than all the wishing in the world.

Flash Fiction

Some stories may not be suitable for children

The Conqueror

By Kristina F. Jordan, M.A.

Gleams. Yes, that's the word, it gleams, I thought. *Maybe even like there's something alive in it, something slimy like an oil slick.*

I felt repulsed, yet unable to stop staring at the bracelet in my employer's jewelry box. Hidden in her boudoir, shining so brightly, I could see myself in its obsidian reflection.

She'll never even miss it! I assured myself, lying with certainty. Did I imagine laughter?

Sparkling like a firelight, I wrapped my fingers around the bracelet, gently rocked it free of the jewelry surrounding it, and pushed some other precious gems back over the newly empty place, attempting to fill and cover my deed. Then I fled.

I ran wildly past the silks and robes I was meant to clean for my mistress, past the floors that beckoned for my calloused hands to polish them, past the doors that had welcomed me so many years before, and into the morning light, feeling dark and dirty inside, but ebullient at the success of my crime.

Wild-eyed and slightly maddened, I arrived before the keeper of an old antique shop.

"Sir, my mistress bought this bracelet from you some time ago, and ever since has wondered about its origin. Can you tell me where it came from? The markings are unique and undecipherable."

The old man stepped from behind the safety of his counter to peer closely into the riveting images dancing within the bracelet's facets.

"Ah yes, of course. This gem came from the estate of one of my closest friends. I know for certain that she bought it in Delphi, Greece, the place of the oracles and all the ancient tales they foretold. Yes, what a find! This is definitely a keeper."

At the word Delphi, I shook and trembled. Feeling faint, I feared I might fall.

Mother had named me Daphne, a Greek name with a nod to an ancient goddess, undoubtedly because I had been conceived during a full moon tryst in the woods with a stranger whose name she never knew.

The police and my mistress will just believe I had been kidnapped, I convinced myself.

As I quickly gathered all of my money and bought a ticket to Greece, I knew, just knew with a certainty beyond belief that I was doing the right thing. This bracelet had been mine, and was now mine again, and no one and nothing could stop me from finding out the truth about it.

Athens was bright and beautiful. I felt right at home, but I knew time was of the essence; I could not gamble on the Spirits staying in my favor forever. So after only one night soaking in the texture of Athens, drinking Retsina with the locals in a delicious bouquet of food and dance, I felt driven to rise early and get myself to the bus that would wind its way up the treacherous mountainside up, up, up to the Oracle of Delphi.

On the ride, I read about the oracles and how they had served kings. But I was no king. I was a bastard child of a wild prostitute taken to bouts of drug abuse and drinking to deaden the pain in her life, a mother who left me with unreliable strangers until the state took me in and left me with paid strangers. Still, inside my deepest fears and grandest yearnings, I felt the tremors of murky hope, a hope that something momentous was about to happen.

When I looked up from my book, I saw a sight that took my breath away. The landscape rose to greet my hungry gaze. I recognized the mountains, folding one into the other, and the clouds the bus was carefully rising above on this long, winding trail.

I've been here before, I thought gleefully, unexpectedly. *I know this place!*

When everyone disembarked to search for trinkets and new memories, I found myself wandering the trails experiencing old memories, fond memories.

Suddenly the Delphi Museum appeared, and something told me I must go inside.

There, I saw a giant beehive turned to stone that felt very familiar, then walked past statues of soldiers and men I felt I knew. Laughing, I shook off the feeling.

Then I entered the main room and saw "The Conqueror." Here stood a statue of a man on a podium, broad of muscular chest, arms as wide as my thigh, a mighty, powerful figure with a thick beard and balding head.

My heart stopped at the sight. I knew this man. I knew him intimately. I knew his body, his strong hands, his feet in his sandals—that presence, that reality. Yes, I knew him. Like a mirrored cloak thrown around us, inside this shadowy place time and space no longer existed, and I felt, I believed, I knew, I had been him. I was "The Conqueror."

I closed my eyes, and all the walls of today melted into yesteryear.

I knew no enemy I did not destroy. What I saw, I took. What I wanted, I took. What I stole, I made laws to keep. No man or woman dared speak against me. No one, no one stood against me. Not without failure. Not without punishment.

Even the young king shook when I bellowed his name. Yes, I was the King of Kings!

I reveled in this time warp, pride and power flooding my soul, changing me, transforming me from the mouse I was into this giant, the man I'd once been.

Terrestrial Landing

By Donna Marie Robb

Terror pulsed through me. We were minutes away from landing on a new planet.

I had spent my entire life on this spaceship, all sixteen years. My parents had been born here, as were my grandparents and great-grandparents. Now, we were going to be thrust from our comfortable home onto a terrifying new world.

From the stories I'd heard, the aliens that dwelled below were hostile creatures who slaughtered one another at whim and thrived on war.

We would arrive as peacekeepers, bringing much needed order. But why did we have to do it? I tried to comfort myself with the fact that their technology was primitive compared to ours. They'd be powerless against us if they chose to attack.

But doubt still gnawed at me.

As I stood, elbow-to-elbow, with my fellow citizens, I peered through the bridge's vast window down at the planet drawing closer, ever closer. It reminded me of the photos I'd seen of our world, the ones my people had left centuries again. It seemed so peaceful from up here, incandescent blue mottled with land masses that peeped out from beneath swirled clouds.

I knew that if the aliens attacked us, we'd be ready. But that realization didn't stop the nerves squirming in my stomach.

"We will be entering the atmosphere shortly," came the

booming voice of our captain. "My crew and I will exit first to make the introductions. The aliens are known to be skittish and primitive. They call themselves humans, and their world is Earth."

The Spice Market

By Diane H. Fisk

Shaking from lack of sleep, Helene entered the exotic Middle Eastern spice market. Her friend Michela told her this market had every spice imaginable, and she could find a cure for her night terrors. Little did she know that the shopkeeper was a vampire in disguise.

"Can you help me please?" she asked the white-faced, dark-haired man name Braun.

He turned and glared at her. Then Braun's eyes softened as he saw how beautiful Helene was.

"But of course, my dear. How may I be of service?"

"I can't sleep. Every night I am tormented by the worst thoughts and night terrors. I must get some sleep or I will go crazy."

"Come. Take my arm. I will show you around my shop. I am certain I have something that will cure you of this problem," he said with a strange accent.

As they walked around the room, Helene shuddered as she felt Braun's hot breath on her neck.

Braun looked at her with hungry eyes, and he held her ever closer as they walked around the room from table to table.

"Ah, this is the one. This spice will cure you of all horrible thoughts. You will only have good ones from the moment you swallow this."

"No, give her the meleconin instead. That will do the trick," yelled Lilo, Braun's wife, from the doorway.

Braun turned.

"Please. One moment. My wife and I need to discuss this matter," he said as he disappeared into the back of the store.

"My dear Braun, if you do not give her the meleconin, I promise to torment you for the rest of your unnatural life," Lilo said.

"But darling, you know the effect this will have on her," he said.

"I do know. She deserves it."

"What do you mean?"

"I saw the way you looked at her, like you want to drink her blood and be married to *her* forever. Well, you can't have her."

Braun paused. He knew Lilo meant what she said, and he knew better than to tangle with her when she was in one of her moods. He grabbed the meleconin.

They returned to the front of the shop where Helene was sampling several spices.

"Here you are, my dear. Take this and you will be cured of night terrors forever."

Helene grabbed the bottle and swallowed its contents without hesitation.

Helene felt her ankles buckle and her legs start to shrink. She was getting smaller and smaller!

"Please help me," yelled Helene.

"Ha, ha, ha. That will teach you to come in here and expect to get cured by strangers," yelled Lilo.

Helene was now the size of a small mouse. She looked up at the huge tables over her head. Every noise sounded much louder than normal. She spoke.

"Why would you do this to me?"

Before they could answer, a handsome prince named Lance entered the shop.

"Have you seen the beautiful lady who came in here several minutes ago?" the prince asked.

"No, sir. The only person I have seen all day is my lovely wife, Lilo," Braun said.

Helene shouted in her biggest voice, "I'm down here! Can you hear me?"

"Do you hear something? I could swear I heard a voice," said Lance.

Braun started to sweat. "No sir. I hear nothing. Is there anything else I can help you with today?"

"No," Lance said. "I need to find that beautiful lady."

"I am sure I have a spice which can help you find the woman that you seek. Here, take this," the shopkeeper said as he handed Lance a bottle.

Lance took one whiff and knocked the bottle out of Braun's hands as it crashed to the floor spilling its contents.

The pungent spice had such a strong smell that it counteracted the effect that the meleconin had on Helene, and she felt herself getting larger. Up, up her body grew, and soon she was her normal size.

"Thank goodness you followed me. I was given a terrible spice that made me shrink. They did it on purpose. These people are horrible!"

"My dear, you are just upset. Of course, no one could possibly do that."

"Please, seize them," pleaded Helene.

Lance grabbed them both and pulled them out of the spice shop into the arms of the police waiting outside.

"We've heard bad reports of this place. We will be very happy to take these creeps off your hands."

Braun and Lilo no longer a threat, Lance gave Helene his arm and they walked into the sunset together.

The Knife

By Lynne Southerland

He was pointing a knife at me. I had just rinsed the soap from my favorite stainless steel pan, the one I boil fresh beans in every morning, when I turned to find him stiff armed and resolute. He had not been his usual self all week, ever since that segment on the Sunday news. We had all watched it together, like we were witnessing the debut of what was going to be a long and successful acting career. After all, he was the star of the segment. They called it "Sunday's Child." Made me think of that rhyme, "but the child who is born on the Sabbath Day, is bonny and blithe and good and gay."

We were all gay as we turned on the television set and munched on the chips we dunked in the salsa I had made special for the occasion. I drank a Coke while he and the other children sipped from juice boxes. We were antsy as we suffered through the last of the real news stories before his big moment.

He enjoyed being the center of attention. He shook his leg, trying to calm his stage fright. I was so happy that he was getting this chance. Now maybe he would find a permanent home with a loving couple who could cultivate his naturally inquisitive nature into a high-achieving member of society. I hoped that the couple who would watch the segment and fall in love with his happy face and athletic body would be black, so he would look at them and see himself.

I had taken him in when he was eighteen months old and

showered him with the love I had given to my own kids, now grown, and the other foster children we had taken in when our nest became empty ten years ago. I relished the first time he spoke, looking at me and saying "Mama." I took pride in his ability to make friends easily and his natural curiosity about the world around him. But I knew it must be hard for him to look at our family and see the brown skin and wavy, black hair that our grandparents carried with them from Mexico. At five years old he was starting to notice these things.

After an endless series of commercials, his segment began. We all clapped with joy when they showed the first shot of him. His smile lit up the screen. I turned in time to see that same look on his face as he stared at himself. They showed footage of him playing on the beach and climbing the monkey bars. The other kids patted him on the back. He was a star—at least in our house.

But then the man's voice narrating the story became serious as he told us, and thousands of people watching the news at home, about how our star had been born in the county jail. In all of our excitement that unpleasant fact might have slipped by us, but the narrator continued to report more heartbreaking information about a mother who was a crack addict and multiple-offender. My mouth fell open. My heart raced. It took too many seconds for me to comprehend the blow being delivered to him. It took me too long to grab the remote and turn the segment off. It was too late to erase this memory from any of our minds.

He was the first to try and save the day. He played the celebrity and boasted how he was the only one who had been on TV. I hoped that he was, as they say about children, resilient. Able to forget a bad taste in his mouth as soon as he put a better one against his tongue. I refused to see how with each passing day he grew quieter, less playful.

***

As I washed the dishes, I asked him to put the dirty napkins in the trash. I heard him say "no" with particular venom in his voice. I put my favorite pan in the dish rack to dry and turned to scold him, discovering the knife in his little hand. I was relieved to see it was only a butter knife. But the anger on his face vibrated through my body, and my knees buckled. I begged him to put the knife down, but he stood his ground. I don't know what would have happened if my husband hadn't walked in.

The knife hit the tile floor with a dull thud and he ran out the back door. My husband held me tight. He did not ask for details. He did not say anything. But I knew what he was thinking.

***

A few days before Christmas, he was taken from our home. I never saw him again. My husband and children were full of anger and fear. I knew they had never seen him as one of us, like I had. I knew there was nothing I could say so that he could stay with us.

Now each Christmas fills me with melancholy. I wonder what ever happened to him. I wonder if he remembers me, the woman he used to call Mama. I wonder if he ever found that couple and made that perfect life I had pictured for him. And I hope the system didn't fail him the way I did.

Redemption

By Nora Rodriguez

She had walked all over town, looking for it in the different shops. Up to now, she'd had no luck. For the most part, this was a quiet town, peaceful even, and for some reason this discouraged her. *Surely a peaceful place had no need for such a thing.* It was contradictory for them to coexist in the same place at the same time.

So the girl decided to give up. She would go home and think of another way to accomplish her goal.

As she was about to leave, she saw the General Store at the corner and walked towards it.

The girl stood at the door before entering; she took a deep breath and went inside. As she closed the door behind her, a little bell rang. There was no one at the counter, so she started to look around. There were all sorts of things: canned food, writing tablets and pencils for school, jars full of candy, hats and fishing gear, among other odds and ends. Behind the counter were shelves full of things. It was there that she saw one with a clear handle-just a toy-and the real one she wanted.

It was dark brown, long and sleek. It hung on a hook pointing up, waiting, quietly waiting.

"I'm here," the girl said.

She knew the storekeeper would not sell it to her. So, just as she had planned, she stole it. She quietly went behind the counter and took it off the hook it was hanging on.

The girl knew stealing was a sin, just as great as the sin she was

157

about to commit. She wanted to redeem herself somehow, so she took out the crystal rosary her grandmother had given her and hung it on the hook. Quietly she walked out of the store. When the shopkeeper came back from his lunch, he noticed a rosary in the same place where his gun used to hang.

With the gun tucked inside her coat, the girl ran home as fast as she could. She felt as if her heart would burst and her head ached. It didn't matter; she must go through with this. She must put an end to her father's beatings and his insults. She couldn't take it anymore; she had to protect herself and her mother.

The girl walked into her parents' room and there he was, lying on the bed. The room was unusually quiet. She tiptoed over to the bed with the gun in front of her, pointing straight at him. As she grew closer, she could see him better. There he was, smelling of alcohol, unshaven, menacing even while he lay still. Her father's eyes were wide open--he looked alive.

But he was dead.

A Week in the Life of an Honesty Queen

By Lucy Ravitch

I hid from the boys in my normal spot for the week. Ben and Vern were walking home from school next to the dilapidated buildings.

"I wish our neighborhood could have a toy store," Vern said.

Ben stayed quiet. I gathered he didn't have much money. Even if there was a toy store, he probably couldn't afford to buy anything.

"Ben, wouldn't a toy store be great?" Vern prodded.

"I guess so," Ben finally replied.

"You don't sound that excited about the idea, Ben. You know, just 'cause you don't have money doesn't mean you can't get anything," Vern smiled.

Ben scrunched his face.

"Huh?"

"You can just take something; the little things that can fit in your pocket always beg to be taken."

This is how I knew that Vern wasn't the best kind of boy. Ben, on the other hand, had something special. Ben didn't reply to Vern, and that's when a silly black cat tried to get me, and I had to run and hide.

Ben saw me and shouted, "Vern, did you see that?"

"No. What?"

"It was a, a bunny. I think."

Just then, my enemy showed up to tempt the boys. He was dressed in a sharp suit that didn't quite fit the neighborhood.

"Well, hello young lads," he said to the boys.

"Hi," Vern replied.

Ben elbowed Vern for talking to a stranger.

The "stranger" was none other than Mr. Dark. In my land he is known as the Dark Wizard.

He continued talking to the boys. "I'm an investor in these parts, and I might be interested in putting in a toy store here. Is that something that would interest you?"

Ben said quickly, "Maybe, Mister. Listen, we gotta go."

He pulled Vern's arm, dragging him away.

I followed them and was not spotted this time.

Vern looked mad.

"What did you do that for?"

"He gave me the creeps, Vern. You saw how he just popped out of nowhere."

The boys said goodbye and went their separate ways for the weekend. I followed Ben to make sure that Mr. Dark didn't go anywhere near him.

***

Ben lived in humble circumstances. I saw that he didn't have a great home life. He lived with an elderly aunt who would watch TV all day long while Ben prepared her breakfast, lunch, and dinner. Ben couldn't cook much, but he was good at getting cereal, heating up soup, and using the microwave.

The weekend went by without Mr. Dark going anywhere near Ben.

But come Monday morning, I saw what Mr. Dark was up to.

***

As Ben met up with Vern to walk to school, they saw Mr. Dark's handiwork—a decked-out toy store in the middle of all the vacant shops. A sign in the window read: Grand Opening Today At 2:00 P.M.

Vern shouted, "Yes! Thank heavens for that weird guy. I can't wait to see what they have this afternoon."

I stayed near this new shop while the boys went to school. All day I watched Mr. Dark conjure up tempting little toys and trinkets for girls and boys to steal, along with big ticket items. He cast spells and whispered to the wind.

I was doing my best to leave clues for all the boys and girls so they would not be deceived. I left notes that said, "Follow your heart," and "Do what's right," but Mr. Dark's minions got to them within five minutes.

***

Vern came with a group of friends that afternoon. Ben trailed behind. Vern's group entered the shop along with several other children from school, but Ben stayed back. I was silently cheering

Ben on. I knew he would do the right thing and not even go into the shop.

Ben looked through the window and stared for several minutes. There was every toy imaginable in the store: balloons, toy planes, stuffed animals, Frisbees, candy. It all must have looked so good to Ben. As he turned to leave, the wind blew a $20 bill onto the front of his jacket.

I ran out and tried to get Ben's attention. He was too interested in the money, though. Ben ran into the shop with me just behind. He went through the aisles and found a gift he treasured.

Ben approached the long line of children waiting to purchase their items. As he stood there he finally noticed me, hopping up and down, pointing at Mr. Dark.

Mr. Dark was talking to a child and trying to shoo me away with his left foot.

Ben's face changed. I could tell he had a change of heart. He put the toy away and walked up to Mr. Dark.

"I can't take this money, Mister."

"It's yours. Go ahead. Buy something," he said softly.

"No, I found it outside your shop, so here you go," Ben said, shoving the bill into Mr. Dark's hand.

Time froze.

Then all at once the scenery shattered and disappeared. The toy store was now a vacant shop filled with empty, dusty boxes, just as it had been days ago.

Mr. Dark transformed back into his normal, unsightly figure, and I resumed my stature, 5'2" tall in a white gown.

Mr. Dark snarled.

"Wilma, you saved that boy, but I got about five kids this time!" he said as he walked out of the store with his briefcase full of children who stole from him.

Ben looked surprised, just as I expected. It happens every time.

I put my arm around Ben and spoke to him all the way back to his house.

"Ben, you have proven yourself to be truly honest. You escaped the jaws of the dark wizard."

***

It was another successful week. Ben proved he was as special as I thought he was and the dishonest kids faced their consequences.

Now, on to wherever Mr. Dark is off to next.

Melrose Avenue Blues

By Lissa Ross

"Welcome to L.A.!" were the first words I heard after landing at LAX from Australia.

I moved to Hollywood and needed a job, so I ended up working for an old ex-mafia couple with a junky store on Melrose Avenue. They constantly argued and bossed me around. My life seemed far away from the dreams of what I thought L.A. would be like. The hours moved way too slowly.

One day, a photographer came by and asked if he could take my photo for a casting agency down the street. I agreed.

When my bosses found out, they were furious, sure it was a rival mafia-owned store that was trying to spy on their merchandise. Needless to say, I was unceremoniously fired and sent home.

That night, the phone rang. It was the casting agency asking me if I'd like to be featured in a large music video they were about to start shooting the next day.

I'm glad to say I never had to work on Melrose Ave again.

The Unique Temptress in a Sea of Emotional Pollution

By Diane Sepulveda Robinson

Delilah was beautiful, slender, and well educated. But she lived in a heartbreaking shadow of doubt, guilt, and shame.

Delilah had an addiction to melancholy. She could not unfetter it, so she used self-deprecating humor to deepen her wounds and punished herself with broken relationships, unemployment, debt and a home filled with her past. Reminders of things, events, and relationships told in photos, articles, and clothing were kept and piled into boxes, files, or drawers. Her closets were stuffed with clothes and shoes she could not let go of.

She knew from watching hoarding TV shows that clutter was a confusing or disorderly state and a possible symptom of compulsive hoarding. Yet her main problem was not necessarily an effluence of hoarding in her home. It wasn't smog or litter or contamination on the wonders of the planet Earth. Like a dark corner, her mind and mental emotions were the real cluttered spaces in her life, hoarded with gloom, obscurity, and shadows.

Delilah became her worst enemy and as she sank into the inner dimensions of her life's journey, she acquired a mindset of clutter. The awareness and alertness of a bright mind had turned into a store of negative thoughts hanging from the ceiling and shelves of her cerebral cortex.

***

While reading the newspaper, she saw an article about a small town with many antique stores not far from where she lived, and she felt the urge to expand her collections.

Delilah drove to the town and stopped in front of one store with a front window display crowded with objects such as toys, books, stuffed animals, dolls, and clocks. With hesitation, she began walking up the rickety steps into the front entrance.

As Delilah walked in, she saw the room was dimly lit with a few overhead lights that cast a soft glow over the large and small objects piled along the walls, ceilings, and floors of the store. The store was polluted with absurd objects in every niche, corridor, and shelf.

Delilah became fearful of the dark and the objects that lurked in the shadows. She turned to run away. Fear and disappointment always prevented her from just "turning on" the lights of truth. Just as she turned, she saw a bright streak of light emanating from the back of the room, hypnotizing her to walk toward it.

As she began walking in the direction of the light, she entered a second room identical to the dark room, only all the objects that hung from every corner, ceiling, shelf, and niche were brightly lit. There were bright and colorful toys, dolls, clocks, and books. Suddenly, she began to feel lighthearted and full of laughter and joy as she became more aware and alert of her surroundings.

In a large dressing mirror, she saw a reflection of herself as a seductive and alluring temptress. Delilah launched into a fearless laugh. Her mind began to lift from that foggy sea of pollution and clutter, changing evil to good, dark to light, sadness to happiness.

Her heart overflowed with love of herself: a beautiful woman. She no longer needed the crutch of old antiques, which made her feel old and unwanted.

Delilah walked outside to feel the warmth of the sun, to see and smell the beauty of nature surrounding her, to hear the birds chirping joyfully and to feel love and gratitude of being alive for this day of discovery.

Was that article in the newspaper the end of a heartbreaking journey of a hoarded mindset? A new path, and a journey of light and childlike freedom of nature?

Delilah no longer felt conflicted within her mind of darkness and emotional pollution. She was now a temptress of light, committed to making a difference and to serving others in appreciation of the beautiful planet earth.

Less Than Shining Armor

By Cacy Duncan

He plummeted toward the planet in advance of an armada large enough to wipe out entire galaxies. But not advanced enough. They were right behind him—80 World Destroyers flanked by 30,000 Oppressors and 500,000 grunt fighter jets!

His little stolen cruiser punched through the atmosphere in a blazing arc of fire and salvation. Only he knew how this poor, defenseless planet could prevail against the coming slaughter. Only he knew the armada's single weakness. There wouldn't be much time after he landed, but he would see to it that the people of this planet had a choice other than extinction.

Alarm lights flashed through the cockpit.

The engines announced their failure with a silence that screamed finality. The power to the ship cut off in the same instant. His visor screen went black.

In the darkness of the shaking cockpit, he pushed every button, flipped every switch, said every prayer he could think of, but the guidance systems, life support, airlock door—all of it responded with cold indifference.

His crummy little stolen cruiser wouldn't come back online. The entry had been too much for the ship he'd stolen from the repair bay of the World Destroyer he'd hitched a ride on.

Well, shit, he thought as he careened toward certain death. *Who's going to save the Earth now?*

All in the Timing

By Kathryn Thornton

Sarah hadn't planned to tell the prom committee that her best friend, Amanda, didn't want to be on the ballot for prom queen. It just came out. Since they were six years old, that had been all that Amanda had wanted. But so had Sarah. Amanda had never let Sarah wear her tiara, never let Sarah be the princess.

When Sarah thought of a prom queen, as she had been programmed by all forms of media, she immediately thought of someone who looked like Amanda—tall, slender yet curvaceous, and blonde. Not someone who was lanky, had mousy brown hair, and dark brown eyes with a smattering of freckles across her nose. Try as she might, she could not picture herself wearing the crown.

Sarah would never win. So why had she done it? It was so easy to tell the lie, but it was going to be impossible to fix. What if Amanda refused to forgive her when she found out the truth?

Maybe when Amanda came to school tomorrow, and the ballots were out with a box for Sarah instead of Amanda, she could say it was a mistake and get away with it. Although Sarah had to tell Sierra Johnson how to spell her name twice, even though they'd been in the same school since first grade.

Sarah's feet dragged along the pavement as she trudged home. She knew as soon as she got home that Amanda would call her to talk about prom. Sarah was actually thankful her parents had taken away her cell phone when she had been caught texting in class by uptight Ms. Lee. Not having a cell phone was going to be a great excuse for why she hadn't texted Amanda immediately about getting on the ballot. Even if she was on her deathbed, Amanda would have wanted to show up to get her name on the prom court ballot.

Sarah stopped short outside of her house. She had arrived later than normal but sooner than she wanted. She could tell her mother that she had laryngitis as an excuse to not let her speak on the phone with Amanda. That might work. But her parents couldn't afford to pay for her to go to the doctor, and her mom would insist if she faked laryngitis. Sarah hadn't even been able to purchase a prom dress yet, and the prom was less than two weeks away.

"Sarah, dear? Why are you sitting out here on the front steps?" her mother asked. "Oh my, your face is so red. Do you feel alright?"

Sarah's mother felt her cheeks and her forehead while scanning her face.

"Amanda's mother said she is quite ill. With all the time you two spend together, you are going straight to bed. We can't be too careful."

The next morning Sarah dragged herself out of bed wondering if she should play the sick card again and stay home. Avoiding Amanda was working so far. If she didn't vote for herself today then she probably wouldn't get any votes at all. *Would people know that? Do they announce the vote totals or just the winner?*

Sarah's mother walked in while she was having her panic attack and decided to keep her home because of her flushed cheeks and wild look in her eyes.

Her mother called the school office to say that Sarah was too sick to come to school.

***

Kelly, the drama department queen, was working in the office and overheard bits of the conversation. The parts she heard were juicy. There was a student who was very sick who wanted to be prom queen but couldn't make it to school to vote or stand up and address the students at assembly today. Kelly needed some philanthropic items to add to her college application, and this was just what she needed. If she made it her mission to help this poor student, it would be a great topic for her essay!

Kelly slipped into the principal's office and saw Sarah Nichol's name on the absence slip. This was the poor soul she was selflessly going to help.

Kelly had unwittingly overheard two different absence phone calls. The principal had not taken the time to write Amanda Keith's absence slip yet.

***

Sarah arrived at school the next day to find a downcast Amanda waiting for her. Sarah smiled weakly and approached cautiously. Amanda had a temper, and if she was aware of what Sarah had done, she would be yelling already.

"I was out sick yesterday and I didn't get to address the senior class to vote 'Amanda for Prom Queen.' I asked if I could do a make-up today and was told all the voting was done yesterday. I can't believe that I was sick on the day of prom court voting. I begged my mom to let me come to school. I will never forgive her for this."

Amanda still looked weak and didn't have any fight in her words; which made Sarah feel even worse. She hugged her friend and gave her a weak smile.

***

Amanda was still hopeful that she would be prom queen because she had heard that Kelly, the junior from the drama department, had given a very moving speech about a sick student. No one could remember the name she had told them to vote for, but Amanda was sure it was her.

When they announced the prom queen, Amanda started walking confidently towards the stage.

***

Sarah stood, mouth agape and frozen with shock. *They said my name?!*

Sarah's smile encompassed her whole face, and the wonderful unfamiliar weight of the crown on her head caused her to stand taller as she waved and thanked her classmates. She especially wanted to thank Kelly for making her secret dream come true.

A Mission From Memory

By Angie Flores

The door rings as I enter the shop, announcing my arrival. I take in the smell of incense and smoke as I clasp my hands behind my back and examine the paraphernalia that align the walls—bottles with twisted necks, which assist the release of poison to their rightful owner, invite the eyes with their unique shapes and colors. A sigh of sorrow escapes through my teeth as I slowly walk along the glass cases.

"This can't be his choice," I pray as I think back to the innocent baby I held in my arms. I had embraced this boy, my nephew, as I watched my sister slowly succumb to a destructive lifestyle, finally slipping into permanent slumber.

As I stop at a poster of Bob Marley and stare at the words "One Love," I am thrown into memories of an abusive father who cared only for his daily dose of liquor and weed, how the reggae music played so loudly in my home to cover the screaming from pain my mother had to endure at the hands of her husband.

A clicking sound pulls me back as a woman enters through a beaded curtain covering the doorway to the back room.

"Hello, Father. How may I help you today?"

I notice her eyes are not completely aligned. She cannot accept reality without chemical substance. A puff of smoke comes from behind the curtains. She is clearly not alone. I pull a picture of a little boy from my pocket and place it on the counter. I look into the woman's face with the serious intention to reach her inner core.

"It has been ten years that I have been looking for this child. I am his uncle. I loved his mother, my sister, dearly. But consequences pulled us apart. She passed and left her son in the care of friends; I have heard they have moved here to this city, unfamiliar as it is to me."

Rustling sounds escape from behind the curtain, distracting me from my speech. I hear movement in the back room. The woman glances over her shoulder and then retrieves the picture to examine it.

"This is one cute child, Father. Must be a shame not to know where this precious puppy is."

Her smile does not fully reach her eyes. I look around at all the posters of cannabis leaves, rock bands with half dressed women, and fornicating couples. This is not comfortable for me. Nor is it foreign.

I remember how I watched my sister whimper under the rage of her own father and the helpless pleading from behind doors left slightly ajar as my father had his way with her.

I swallow hard to hold back my pain. I know I should not be in such an environment of sin while I have pledged my life to God, but my mission is not complete. I find my feet are encased in concrete as I cannot bring myself to leave the store.

The woman is regarding me with the eyes of a snake, knowing I am not a customer, suspicious nonetheless. I pick up a pack of mints and examine it.

"I want to talk to him, for just a moment. I want him to know that there is family still around. A blood line for him to follow. I don't want him to feel as though he has to give in to his surroundings."

The woman is agitated, wanting to get back to her prior engagement.

"Well, he will be a lucky boy, if you find him. Listen, Father, if you are just here to look around, enjoy yourself. Call me if you need me. I can't help you with what you seek."

I drink in her expression of frustration as she excuses herself through the beaded curtain. I feel dejected, knowing that I finally came close to my finding my nephew, but hadn't succeeded. Reluctantly, I leave the store.

Walking with heavy weight past the store front, I hear footsteps coming up close behind me. A sudden hand is placed on my shoulder and spins me around, facing familiar eyes. A young man looks into my eyes and confesses.

"Forgive me, Father, for I have sinned."

Doom's Homecoming

By Stacy Anderson

Gone are the days of Doom. Everything left is in shades of grey. When the Doom left, so did the color, but it was humanity's choice—peace and anonymity rather than chaos, stillness rather than fear. That was the trade-off people made to rid themselves of the Doom.

Then came the little girl, born with pink hair that all could see, half-human, half-Doom, a remnant from a past all wanted to forget. Where she came from, no one knew, but whenever they looked at her, their old fear returned. Many were blinded by these fears, and hatred for the little girl grew.

Finally, one day the council of elders voted to rid the kingdom of Curlyation of this reminder of the Doom. The little girl was to be burned at the stake. She was tied up, a bonfire built around her, yet she uttered no words. Flames lapped around her, and still she remained calm until a little weeping escaped from her chest. The weeping grew louder, piercing onlookers' ears. Some turned away and covered their ears, while others looked bewildered by what they had done.

One little boy could take the weeping no longer and ran into the fire to free the little girl. When he tried to leap through the fire, he was knocked back by a big explosion and fell unconscious.

When he woke up, everything was pitch black.

He could not tell if he was blind, but he could feel the Doom around him. When he could take it no more, lights flashed around him in brilliant colors, colors that awed him.

He looked to his left, and saw that nothing was left of the bonfire. The pink-haired girl was gone, turned to ashes of grey. To his right, the people who had cowered and covered their ears had turned to stone in their exact stance of fear.

All that was left in the middle of the bonfire circle was a little pink butterfly. It flapped its wings, flew over to him, landed on his shoulder and sang, "Welcome home."

Poetry

I Have Sickle Cell

By Christal Terry

My name is Wayne.

I am sick.

I have to go to the hospital.

I have sickle cell anemia.

It causes pain in my joints.

I try to be strong,

But sometimes I cry.

It's okay, though; the doctors and nurses are nice.

They give me medicine to take away the pain.

Soon I am ready to go home again.

I look and feel better, but still I am different from my friends.

Sometimes it's a bore,

Not able to play sports.

I read books instead and make stories in my head.

Don't tell anyone, but my sickle cell is really a superpower.

At night while I sleep, I fight evil monsters.

One is named Malaria.

Malaria is a very mean monster.

He likes to take people away from their families.

I am protected from him by my sickle powers.

I'm the only one who can fight the evil monster and keep people safe from harm.

Everyone sleeps well,

Including me.

I have the best dreams ever.

Appendices

Appendix A: The Four Literary Forms

Why Four Literary Forms?

We encouraged our writers to use one of four literary forms for each of their pieces—essay, flash fiction, picture book manuscript, or poetry. The forms were selected for their brevity and uniquely different characteristics.

Most of the "Writers on Writing" pieces were completed in poem and essay form, while the "Shopping for Stories" pieces skewed towards flash fiction and picture books.

We elected to simplify the first part of the anthology and split the authors' work between poetry and prose, while the second part identifies at least one example from each of the four literary forms.

Every CBW-LA Writing Day Workshop attendee was given the following handouts to use as a reference throughout the day.

HANDOUT 1:
ESSAY

What is an essay?

• A nonfiction piece of writing (usually prose) written from the author's personal point of view.

• The purpose of an essay is to make a point. It aims to support a particular claim.

• The author makes his point in an interesting and catchy manner.

• The essay has a thesis, statement, or theory that the author is promoting.

• The usual goal in writing an essay is to inform, persuade, or convince the reader to change their way of thinking or adopt new ideas.

Four Major Types of Essays

There are four major types of essays, depending on the writer's ultimate goal.

1. Descriptive

• The goal of a descriptive essay is to paint a picture with words.

• Here, a writer aims to convey a deeper meaning to the reader using description. For example, an author may discuss the real meaning of love or loss by describing a particular person, place, object, experience, or memory in his essay.

• Descriptive essays not only appeal to the senses through the use of colorful and powerful words, but they also appeal to the reader's emotions.

2. Expository

• The goal of an expository essay is to convey information or to explain, define, and illustrate a topic.

• Often in an expository essay, the author uses a lot of facts, examples, and even statistics to support his topic.

• In an expository essay, the author might compare and contrast two things, talk about a cause and effect relationship, or, in the case of a "How To" essay, simply explain how a process is done.

3. Narrative

• The purpose of a narrative essay is to tell a story about a real-life experience.

• In a narrative essay, the author writes in the first-person point of view.

• In telling his personal story through the narrative essay, the author encourages the reader to relate to his own experience or to learn something from his story.

4. Persuasive

• The purpose of a persuasive essay is to convince a reader to accept the author's opinion or recommendation.

• Unlike the expository essay, which only means to convey information, the persuasive essay means to change the reader's point of view so that it aligns with the author's.

• In order to persuade the reader to accept his recommendation, an author must use facts, figures, examples, logic, and reason to build his case.

• In a persuasive essay, the author presents all sides of the case but also communicates in a clear manner why one side is more correct than the others.

How to Write an Essay

1. Decide what your topic will be.

2. Figure out your thesis statement, or the main point you are trying to get across.

3. Prepare an outline of your essay by writing down the main point and the other supporting sub-points of your topic.

4. Write out these main points and sub-points in organized paragraphs. Start with an introduction of your main thought and end with your conclusion.

HANDOUT 2:
FLASH FICTION

What is flash fiction?

• Flash fiction is a short form of storytelling. It is a complete story told in 1000 words or less.

• Other names for flash fiction include microfiction, short short story, sudden fiction, prosetry, and postcard fiction.

• Flash fiction stories are complete in that they have a beginning, middle, and end. They also include the usual story elements of character, conflict, dialogue, setting, and plot.

Four Major Elements of Flash Fiction

1. Character

• Flash fiction requires one major character and, at most, at two other characters.

• Character doesn't only refer to sentient beings. You can also do a flash fiction piece on two inanimate objects. For example, you can write a story about a conversation between the fridge and the microwave.

2. Conflict

• This is the main element that drives the plot of the story.

• A flash fiction's conflict is basically what ramps up the tension of the story. It can be the usual conflict of man vs. man, man vs. himself, or man vs. nature.

• The conflict can be physical, mental, or emotional.

3. Setting

• This is where the story takes place. It usually requires only a one sentence description, or even a simple phrase like "on a battlefield," "in the kitchen," or "at the local gym."

• Sometimes the title can also give a clue as to where the action is taking place

4. Resolution

• The resolution shows how the conflict is resolved or concluded.

• Often in flash fiction, the conclusion is an unexpected twist.

How to Write Flash Fiction

As in any type of fiction, flash fiction stories have a beginning, middle and end.

Beginning

• Flash fiction stories usually begin in the middle of the action. The readers are introduced to the conflict right away.

• The reader must also have a sense of the setting and the main character within the first few lines of the story.

• As an author, you may choose to focus on one powerful image to paint a picture of your story without using up too many words. For example, the image of a war-torn village or a ship in a storm.

Middle

• In the middle of a flash fiction story, the conflict is illustrated through the plot. The actions, feelings, thoughts and dialogues of the main character further expound on the plot.

• Use references to a common story so you can save even more words. Mention historical events, famous literary stories, and so on so your reader can make their own inferences about your story.

End

• The end should show the resolution of the conflict.

• As an author, you must make sure the reader cannot predict your ending. Use an unexpected twist to drive home the point at the end of the story.

Sample Flash Fiction

There are many wonderful examples of flash fiction available online and in literary magazines. Read Sisterly Love by Vic Errington below for one sample of flash fiction, reprinted under Creative Commons.

We also shared the following flash fiction with our Writing Day attendees: With One Wheel Gone Wrong by A.M. Holmes (260 words: www.oprah.com/omagazine/Micro-Fiction-Short-Stories-from-Famous-Writers/1), At Confession by Harvey Stanbrough (55 words), and At the Autopsy by Ross Lesko (56 words).

Sisterly Love

By Vic Errington

There she is. That's four times now.

She first came at noon on Monday. Soldiers scrambled for cover. The old woman stood naked, gazing vacantly into the Green Zone. Western soldiers shouted in Arabic -

"Put your hands in the air and drop to your knees."

I had watched as the woman remained silent, unmoving, unnerving, in the dusty Baghdad sunlight. Then the Muezzin called midday Adhan, interrupting the standoff.

"Allahu Akbar" he sang.

Brothers emerged from buildings in response to the call for prayer. Ignoring their disturbed sister they shuffled away from the scene. The soldiers stayed still, eyes fixed on their strange visitor. Wearing only the suit God gave her she could hardly hide anything on her person. They must follow procedure. Then a group of women arrived.

"Mufeeda ... Mufeeda," they cried.

Mufeeda's relatives apologised to the soldiers, explaining her mental illness and her wanderings from the institution that cares for her. They slipped a Burqa over her and led her away.

She returned on Tuesday at the same time. Naked Mufeeda stood peering past the guardhouse into the depths of the military complex. The soldiers took cover and waited while someone made a phone call. Relatives arrived looking embarrassed. The soldiers wandered over and pleasantries were exchanged. Mufeeda was clothed and led away.

On Wednesday they were expecting her. Two soldiers came out, covered her with a blanket and guided her gently to the guardhouse to wait for collection.

Today, as the sun reaches its zenith, she is back. The soldiers greet her with their blanket, though their patience is waning. Something really must be done about this.

Suddenly Mufeeda collapses. She falls heavily onto her face. Soldiers rush to her. One speaks hurriedly into his radio. An ambulance emerges from within the Green Zone. Mufeeda is stretchered into the back, the vehicle performs a quick u-turn, and returns to the heart of the NATO labyrinth.

"Allahu Akbar ..."

I take my iPhone and smile. Our psychologists are brilliant. Four consecutive days they had said. No more, no less. Visiting time was my idea. The distraction is not without irony. Our scientists' electronic body implants are sheer genius, and our cosmetic surgeons deserve much credit.

After the two minutes advised by our logistics expert, I tap the numbers and listen. I hear the answer outside and my heart swells. Mufeeda has made her little brother proud.

(399 words. Published by Weaponizer)

HANDOUT 3:
PICTURE BOOK MANUSCRIPT

What is a picture book?

- Picture books are stories for children meant to be read aloud.

- Picture book stories range from 500–1000 words.

- Picture books are usually comprised of 32 pages.

- In a picture book, the illustrations are important as they tell part of the story.

Five Common Types of Picture Books

1. Board Book

- Ages newborn–2.

- Printed on cardboard pages to withstand the handling of younger children.

- Very few words, often focused on nouns or routines.

2. Concept Book

- Ages 2–8.

- Concept books introduce children to basic themes like the alphabet, colors, counting, shapes, etc.

3. Easy Reader

- Ages 4–8.

- Easy Reader books are structured like chapter books but use limited vocabulary.

4. Non-Fiction

- Ages 3–12.

- Non-fiction books introduce children to new subjects in a creative, factual manner.

- Generally complemented by photos rather than illustrations.

5. Wordless

- Ages 2–12.

- The story is told completely through images or pictures.

- A wordless picture book may encourage dialogue or imaginative play between parent and child, or allow the child to narrate and create.

How to Write a Picture Book

A picture book, like any other story contains the usual essential elements of fiction:

- Character
- Conflict
- Setting
- Plot

Author Eve Bunting recommends the following formula: "Will (name of main character) be able to (whatever you want him/her to do), despite (conflict), despite (conflict), and despite (conflict) . . . and in so doing, will he/she learn (lesson)?"

In order to help flesh out your story, you can ask yourself the following questions:

1. What is your story about?

You must be able to state your idea or storyline in one sentence.

2. How does the story begin?

In one sentence, describe how your story begins.

3. What is your main character's problem?

What is the one obstacle your main character has to overcome by the end of the story?

4. Will kids be able to relate to your story?

a. Is your story too preachy?

b. Is the central theme of your story something that kids of appropriate ages and reading levels can relate to?

c. Does the main kid character resolve the problem on her own, without the help of an adult?

5. Is your story's pacing done so that the reader is encouraged to turn the page?

Your lines should end in an exciting cliffhanger. You can accomplish this by making sure you have correctly figured out the page breaks.

6. Can the other half of your story be told in pictures?

Your story should have illustrative possibilities. The illustrator should be able to come up with a variety of illustrations based on your words.

HANDOUT 4:
POETRY

What is poetry?

• It's easy to recognize poetry because unlike prose, which is written in complete blocks of paragraphs, poetry is organized into lines.

• Unlike prose, which often speaks to the logical part of our minds through explanation or description, poetry speaks most directly to the reader's emotions.

• Poetry is a literary form that communicates ideas by using the elements of language itself—the way the words sound and the way they look on the page.

• Poems tend to have many layers of meanings. Readers of poetry will respond emotionally to a poem not only because of what the words are actually saying, but because of what the words are making the reader feel or imagine.

Poem Structure

• Poems are made up of lines and stanzas, not sentences and paragraphs.

• Lines are grouped together to form stanzas. Just like each paragraph in prose conveys one idea, stanzas are used to illustrate ideas.

• A poet can use the following aspects of poetry to affect the readers experience, depending on what emotions or ideas he wishes to convey:

1. Length of the poetic lines.

Shorter poetic lines will speed up the way people read, while longer lines will slow down their reading speed

2. Line breaks, or where each line will end.

This affects the way a poem sounds because each reader will always have a slight pause at the end of each line. The words at the end of the line are usually emphasized when reading because it is the last thing a reader sees before he moves on to the next line.

3. Form.

The way a poem looks on a page will also affect the way the reader interprets the poem.

Lines that are shorter, with lots of white space, may appear lighter or more delicate. Longer lines packed together may make the poem seem "heavier" in the readers' minds. For example, if your poem is about the freedom a bird experiences in flight, your poem should look visually light and the lines should feel bouncy or airy. If you're writing a poem of loss, however, then you need lines that feel heavy or slow.

How to Write Poetry

1. Just like in free writing, forget about form and structure for a while and just let the words flow.

2. Once you've written everything down, re-read your poem and ask yourself the following questions:

    a. Content: What is my poem really about?

    b. Tone: What mood, feeling, or emotion do I want to encourage in the reader?

    c. Ideas: Are there certain words or phrases that I want to highlight in the reader's mind?

    d. Speed: Do I want the lines to flow more quickly or slowly? Are there areas in the poem that need to be quicker or slower?

3. Revise and edit your poem based on your answers above.

Popular Types and Examples of Poetry

Acrostic

The first letters of each line spell out a word, which is usually what the poem is about.

Example

Elizabeth it is in vain you say "Love not"—thou
sayest it in so sweet a way: In vain those words from
thee or L.E.L. Zantippe's talents had enforced so
well: Ah! if that language from thy heart arise,
Breath it less gently forth—and veil thine eyes.

Endymion, recollect, when Luna tried To cure his
love—was cured of all beside—His follie—pride—and
passion—for he died.

—Edgar Allan Poe, "An Acrostic"

Cinquain

A cinquain is a poem made up of five lines. Each line has a certain
number of syllables and a specific topic or idea. There are many
forms of cinquains, but the most popular involves the following
pattern:

- Line 1: Title (usually a noun)—2 syllables
- Line 2: (Description) Adjectives that describe the title—4
syllables
- Line 3: (Action) or three words that tell the reader more about
the subject of the poem—6 syllables
- Line 4: (Feeling) words that show emotion about the subject
of the poem—8 syllables
- Line 5: Title (or a synonym for the title)—2 syllables

Example

Look up...
From bleakening hills
Blows down the light, first breath
Of wintry wind...look up, and scent
The snow!

—Adelaide Crapsey, "Snow"

Couplet

A couplet is a poem made up of two lines. Each line has the same meter and ends in words that rhyme with each other. Couplets are often humorous or funny; sometimes they're a part of a larger poem as in a sonnet.

Example

```
You still shall live, such virtue hath my pen,
Where breath most breathes, even in the mouths of
men.
```

—Shakespeare, "Sonnet 81"

Diamante

A poem made up of seven lines that are in a diamond shape. It was invented by Iris M. Tiedt in 1969. Search for "Rocks" by Iris M. Tiedt in *A New Poetry Form: The Diamante* for the example shared with Writing Day attendees.

Similar to the cinquain, each line of the diamante has a specific number of words and topic/part of speech:

- Line 1: 1 Noun (Subject)
- Line 2: 2 Adjectives
- Line 3: 3 Verbs
- Line 4: 4 Nouns
- Line 5: 3 Verbs
- Line 6: 2 Adjectives
- Line 7: 1 Noun (Synonym for subject)

Free Verse

A poem without rules of form, meter, rhyme or rhythm.

Example


```
i carry your heart with me(i carry it in
my heart)i am never without it(anywhere
i go you go,my dear;and whatever is done
by only me is your doing,my darling)
                                        i fear
no fate(for you are my fate,my sweet)i want
no world(for beautiful you are my world,my true)
and it's you are whatever a moon has always meant
and whatever a sun will always sing is you

here is the deepest secret nobody knows
(here is the root of the root and the bud of the bud
and the sky of the sky of a tree called life;which
grows
higher than soul can hope or mind can hide)
and this is the wonder that's keeping the stars apart

i carry your heart(i carry it in my heart)
```

—ee cummings, "I carry your heart with me"

Haiku

An ancient Japanese form of poetry with three lines and a fixed number of syllables. Haiku don't rhyme, and the topics often deal with nature.

- Line 1: 5 Syllables
- Line 2: 7 Syllables
- Line 3: 5 Syllables

Example

```
From time to time
The clouds give rest
To the moon-beholders.
```

—Bashō

Limerick

A poem made up of five lines with the pattern AABBA. The first, second and fifth lines rhyme with each other, while the third and fourth lines rhyme together.

Example

```
There was an Old Man with a beard
Who said, 'It is just as I feared!
Two Owls and a Hen,
Four Larks and a Wren,
Have all built their nests in my beard!
```

—Edward Lear

Minute Poem

A rhyming poem made up of 12 lines of 60 syllables written in iambic meter, developed in the late 1960s by Poet Laureate Verna Lee Hinegardner. Search "I Need Someone" by Linda Newman to read the sample poem we shared with Writing Day attendees. A minute poem consists of 3 stanzas with the following rhyme scheme: AABB, CCDD, EEFF. Each stanza has the following syllabic pattern:

- Line 1—8 syllables
- Line 2—4 syllables
- Line 3—4 syllables
- Line 4—4 syllables

Narrative Poem

This poem tells a story. Often they are very long. Examples of narrative poems include the epic and the ballad.

Example

```
The buzz saw snarled and rattled in the yard
And made dust and dropped stove-length sticks of
wood,
Sweet-scented stuff when the breeze drew across it.
And from there those that lifted eyes could count
Five mountain ranges one behind the other
Under the sunset far into Vermont.
And the saw snarled and rattled, snarled and rattled,
As it ran light, or had to bear a load.
```

And nothing happened: day was all but done.
Call it a day, I wish they might have said
To please the boy by giving him the half hour
That a boy counts so much when saved from work.
His sister stood beside him in her apron
To tell them 'Supper.' At the word, the saw,
As if to prove saws know what supper meant,
Leaped out at the boy's hand, or seemed to leap—
He must have given the hand. However it was,
Neither refused the meeting. But the hand!
The boy's first outcry was a rueful laugh,
As he swung toward them holding up the hand
Half in appeal, but half as if to keep
The life from spilling. Then the boy saw all—
Since he was old enough to know, big boy
Doing a man's work, though a child at heart—
He saw all was spoiled. 'Don't let him cut my hand
off—
The doctor, when he comes. Don't let him, sister!'
So. But the hand was gone already.
The doctor put him in the dark of ether.
He lay and puffed his lips out with his breath.
And then—the watcher at his pulse took fright.
No one believed. They listened to his heart.
Little—less—nothing!—and that ended it.
No more to build on there. And they, since they
Were not the one dead, turned to their affairs.

—Robert Frost, "Out, Out—"

Quatrain

A rhyming poem with four lines. There are different rhyme patterns for the quatrain: AABB, ABAB, ABBA, ABCB

Example

```
Tyger Tyger, burning bright,
In the forests of the night;
What immortal hand or eye,
Could frame thy fearful symmetry?

In what distant deeps or skies.
Burnt the fire of thine eyes?
On what wings dare he aspire?
What the hand, dare seize the fire?

And what shoulder, & what art,
Could twist the sinews of thy heart?
And when thy heart began to beat,
What dread hand? & what dread feet?

What the hammer? what the chain,
In what furnace was thy brain?
What the anvil? what dread grasp,
Dare its deadly terrors clasp!

When the stars threw down their spears
And water'd heaven with their tears:
Did he smile his work to see?
Did he who made the Lamb make thee?
```

```
Tyger Tyger burning bright,
In the forests of the night:
What immortal hand or eye,
Dare frame thy fearful symmetry?
```

—William Blake, "Tyger, Tyger"

Shape Poem and Concrete Poem

A visual poem, written in such a way that it forms a visible picture on the page. The shape of the poem reflects its subject. We shared "The Quill" and "The Bird" by modern poet Ernesto Santiago with workshop attendees. Both can be located online using Google.

Sonnet

A poem with 14 lines that combine two other types of poetry. The sonnet begins with three quatrains and ends with a couplet.

Example

```
Shall I compare thee to a summer's day?
Thou art more lovely and more temperate:
Rough winds do shake the darling buds of May,
And summer's lease hath all too short a date:
Sometime too hot the eye of heaven shines,
And often is his gold complexion dimm'd;
And every fair from fair sometime declines,
By chance or nature's changing course untrimm'd;
But thy eternal summer shall not fade
Nor lose possession of that fair thou owest;
Nor shall Death brag thou wander'st in his shade,
```

```
When in eternal lines to time thou growest:
So long as men can breathe or eyes can see,
So long lives this and this gives life to thee.
```

—William Shakespeare, "Sonnet 18"

Appendix B: Workshop Resources

Organizations for Children's Book Writers

Children's Book Writers of Los Angeles (www.cbw-la.org)
Society of Children's Book Writers and Illustrators
(www.scbwi.org)

Recommended Internet Research*

Poetry

www.creative-writing-now.com/definition-of-poetry.html

www.pbs.org/newshour/extra/features/jan-
june00/poetryboxformexamples.html

www.shadowpoetry.com/resources/wip/epitaph.html

www.shadowpoetry.com/resources/wip/minute.html

Picture Book Manuscripts

picturebookden.blogspot.com/2012/03/what-is-picture-book-
linda-strachan.html

www.prattlibrary.org/locations/children/index.aspx?id=4116

www.marisamontes.com/writing_picture_books.htm

tracymarchini.com/2011/02/14/9-factors-that-make-a-picture-
book-successful

Essays

daphne.palomar.edu/handbook/whatisanessay.htm

www.time4writing.com/writing-resources/types-of-essays

lklivingston.tripod.com/essay

grammar.about.com/od/classicessays/CLASSIC_ESSAYS.htm

Flash Fiction

www.writing-world.com/fiction/flash.shtml

www.fictionfactor.com/guests/flashfiction.html

www.flash-fiction-world.com/what-is-flash-fiction.html

www.flash-fiction-world.com/how-to-write-flash-fiction.html

www.guardian.co.uk/books/2012/may/14/how-to-write-flash-fiction

www.thereviewreview.net/publishing-tips/flash-fiction-whats-it-all-about

www.heelstone.com/meridian/meansarticle1.html

www.pifmagazine.com/vol13/essentials.htm

www.writing-world.com/fiction/popek.shtml

*Note: These URLs are valid as of October 2013 and were distributed to Writing Day 2013 participants. Internet listings are subject to change. The links above have been useful to CBW-LA founder Nutschell Windsor. This list is not meant to be an exhaustive list of quality references for children's book writers.

Author Bios

CBW-LA Writing Anthology 2013

CBW-LA Writing Day 2013 Anthology Authors

Stacy Yamaoka Anderson

Stacy Yamaoka Anderson resides in Southern California with her husband, daughter, and Stella, the dog. She enjoys taking Stella to the dog beach, or along for a car ride.

Stacy blogs at StacyYamaoka.com and is on Twitter @stacyyamaoka

Tiffani Barth

Tiffani Barth is an active member of SCBWI and a board member of CBW-LA. She lives in North Hollywood, where she writes YA and middle grade novels. When not writing she can usually be found in a movie theater watching the latest blockbuster or planning her next hiking adventure.

Cacy Duncan

A resident of Inglewood, CA, Cacy Duncan likes writing about aliens, monsters, and superpowers. She likes reading and watching "junk" about aliens, monsters, and superpowers too. She hopes to one day own a t-shirt with an alpaca wearing an Afro on it. If she ever got a puppy, she would name him Kiba. She can occasionally be found on Twitter @WineAri.

Abi Estrin

Abi Estrin writes fantasy/science fiction young adult novels. She is an SCBWI member, produced screenwriter, and playwright. Her novel Stricken won the SCBWI-LA regional Sue Alexander grant. Abi has an M.F.A. in Screenwriting from the American Film Institute and wrote the animated adaptation of Ben Hur (2003) starring the voice of Charlton Heston. She's also had several screenplays optioned by directors.

When she's not drinking coffee and typing away at a new writing project, Abi works as a horse trainer and hunter/jumper riding instructor. She lives with her fiancé and two cats in the hills of Los Angeles.

Diane H. Fisk

Diane H. Fisk is a former public school music teacher. Now living in Los Angeles, she writes stories for young adults and children, as well as screenplays and country music. Diane belongs to SCBWI, CBW-LA, NSAI, TAXI, and S.A.G. She can be found on Facebook at www.facebook.com/Diane.Fisk.37.

Angie Flores

Angie Flores was born and raised in Hollywood. A firm believer in fairy tales, Angie met her Prince Charming after college, and he became her happily ever after. Now she calls the South Bay home, along with her husband and three boys.

Angie's boys inspired her love of writing children's stories and picture books. She has over 20 stories waiting to be discovered. Angie has also written two television pilots, scripts for on-air radio announcements, and a movie script. Currently a part-time human resources manager, she writes handbooks, policies and procedures, and marketing materials.

Angie loves to travel, make jewelry, and roller skate on the beach. Insomnia usually brings her the time to write her stories. Angie has spoken to middle school writing classes on the journey of a story and finding motivation.

Angie serves on the CBW-LA Board of Directors as Marketing and Fundraising Manager.

Glenn Jason Hanna

Glenn Jason Hanna is a Brooklyn-born, Long Island-raised Los Angeles resident who likes baseball, board games, baseball, writing, baseball, the Mets, and baseball. He writes and illustrates picture books, middle grade novels, and has started a YA novel bordering on new adult.

Kristina F. Jordan, M.A.

Kristina F. Jordan has lived in New York City, San Francisco, London, Athens, Cairo, Jerusalem, Philadelphia, and Los Angeles, and loves how people the world over are all so very different while also exactly the same.

She holds a management degree from the USC Annenberg School for Communication.

Kristina has written many scripts. She worked on the staff of LA Law and also wrote, produced, and directed "Peas In A Pod." She loves how it feels to put inspiration to paper, creating characters and their stories. She is enjoying exploring writing for children. Find her at www.facebook.com/Kristina.Jordan.3998

Lucy Ravitch

Lucy Ravitch is a picture book/novelty book author who loves to teach. With a background in elementary education, she shares her love of learning wherever she goes. Lucy is a full-time mother, writer, and blogger living in Southern California. Her math resource blog, www.kidsmathteacher.com, offers free hands-on math activities for anyone who teaches children. Her social links can be found there.

Lucy is the Secretary for CBW-LA and active SCBWI member. She is enthusiastic about writing and learning and has a positive attitude. Writing is a process, and she is grateful for everyone that has helped her become more refined along her writing journey!

Donna Marie Robb

Donna Marie Robb works as a children's librarian and enjoys traveling to exotic foreign countries with her husband, Ron Atmur. She has published several short stories in literary magazines such as Wild Violet, Femspec, and Tales of the Talisman. She has also reviewed children's books for School Library Journal and recently completed a young adult novel.

Diane Sepulveda Robinson

Diane Sepulveda Robinson is a descendant of early Alta California landowners in southern California, San Pedro, and Rancho de los Palos Verdes. She is writing a nonfiction book about her family's history. A retired South Bay police officer, Diane also uses her 35 years of experience to write books on careers in law enforcement and self defense.

Diane serves as Palos Verdes Library District Trustee Secretary. She is a board member with Peninsula Seniors, a member of the American Association of University Women (AAUW), Daughters of the Revolution (DAR), and a member of CBW-LA. Her interests include oil painting and setting up self-defense video presentations.

Nora Rodriguez

Nora Rodriguez lives in the city of Lynwood with her husband of eighteen years and their three sons. She is currently a teacher for LAUSD. Nora enjoys reading, watching old movies, and, of course, writing. Her goal is to someday become a successful author in both the English and Spanish speaking markets.

Lissa Ross

Lissa Ross is an Australian writer living in Los Angeles. After traveling the globe playing music, surfing, and filmmaking, Lissa is now writing her first novel, Alias Jet Girl and the Dolphin Rescue. She is on Facebook at www.facebook.com/jetgirlbook.

Lynne Southerland

Lynne Southerland learned about storytelling surreptitiously from the top of the family staircase as she listened to a true raconteur, her father, weaving words and pauses in perfect intervals that captivated his listeners, including her.

After receiving her B.A. in Comparative Literature, she traveled to Los Angeles, jumping head first into the storytelling world of filmmaking. Lynne's creative journey has taken her from editing to producing to directing and writing. She co-directed Mulan 2, the sequel to the beloved Disney feature about the legendary Chinese heroine. Earlier, she provided creative leadership as producer on such projects as Disney's An Extremely Goofy Movie, HBO's acclaimed multicultural series Happily Ever After, Fairy Tales for Every Child, and Paramount's animated feature Bebe's Kids.

Ten years ago the Muse tapped Lynne on the shoulder and invited her to become an author. Her inspirational picture book manuscript is called Baby's Breath: A Fable About Remembering Who You Are. Her fascination with Aboriginal Australian culture inspired her first YA novel, In the All at Once Time.

Check out her website: showingup.net.

Christal Terry

Christal Terry resides in Hawthorne, CA. She is mother to a seven-year-old boy and currently works as a preschool teacher. Christal is a member of CBW-LA as well as the Greater Los Angeles Writer's Society.

Kathryn Thornton

Kathryn Thornton is a New Hampshire native living in Southern California with her wonderful, supportive family, which includes two adopted rescue dogs. She writes contemporary and new adult fiction. She is inspired by her family, friends, music, art, nature, and all the crazy things that make life wonderful.

An active member in the Children's Book Writers of Los Angeles (CBW-LA), she published two pieces in the CBW-LA Anthology. For more information, visit www.facebook.com/KathrynThornton and KATloveswriting.blogspot.com.

Cameron S. Ulyate

Cameron S. Ulyate grew up in California. As a kid, Cameron could be found climbing mountains or kayaking in the ocean when he had free time from play rehearsals.

As an author, he loves writing about adventures that he never read as a kid. And he loves to break the rules. Who said wizard pirates can't ride mechanical dinosaurs?

In the past, Cameron worked with an AAR literary agent on multimedia marketing. He has also worked for several acting agencies and promoted environmental ad campaigns.

CBW-LA Writing Day 2013 Anthology Authors

Editor Bios

CBW-LA Writing Anthology 2013

Alana Garrigues

Alana Garrigues is a freelance journalist and creative nonfiction author. Originally from Portland, Oregon, she now lives the sunshine life in Redondo Beach with her husband and identical twin daughters.

Alana is an avid traveler, meticulous researcher, terrible housecleaner, incessant daydreamer, nature lover, and dabbler of all things art-related.

She is the Publications Editor for CBW-LA and author of the Writercize blog where she posts original writing prompts for writers, students and teachers (writercize.blogspot.com). She is also a member of the Association for Writers and Writing Programs (AWP).

Visit www.alanagarrigues.com for more information. Also on Facebook at www.facebook.com/AlanaGarriguesWrites and Twitter @alanagarrigues.

Editor Bios

CBW-LA Writing Anthology 2013

Nutschell Anne Windsor

Nutschell (pronounced new-shell and not nut-shell) Windsor is a middle grade/young adult fantasy writer who hails from the Philippines and now lives in sunny Los Angeles. She is President of CBW-LA and an SCBWI-L.A. board member.

Nutschell founded Children's Book Writers of Los Angeles (www.cbw-la.org) in 2010 with the hope of sharing writing knowledge with fellow children's book writers in the area. Following a BA in Psychology from the University of the Phillipines, Nutschell became an English teacher at Miriam College High School. Currently, she works as an accounting clerk.

Nutschell's experiences have turned her into a detail-oriented, organized planner, and she uses these skills to teach and facilitate workshops and critique sessions for CBW-LA.

A Jane-of-all-Trades, Nutschell's interests include photography, traveling, sketching, playing the guitar and drums, playing basketball, badminton, billiards, and singing in the shower. She also practices the Filipino martial art of Escrima and bakes yummy desserts.

She is also an active member of the blogging community. She shares writing tips, techniques, and reports on various writing events at www.thewritingnut.com and on Twitter @nutschell.

Acknowledgements

The writers of the CBW-LA Writing Day Anthology took an incredible journey both together and along each of their perspective paths. We would like to thank all of our anthology writers, along with the friends, family, and teachers who gave each of you that extra push towards fulfilling your writing dream. To the spouses and children, we know it takes patience to live with a writer, and for that we thank you.

To Erin Elizabeth Long, thank you for your watchful eye and swift magic in editing this anthology.

To Keela Jacks, thank you for creating a stunning visual image to illustrate the concept behind story sprouts as our book cover designer.

To Rachel Morgan, thank you for formatting both the print and electronic versions of this book. We could not have gone to print without you.

To Maiko Morotani, thank you for believing in this pipe dream of a non-profit, for your emotional and financial support, and unbeatable pancake breakfasts. Your generous donation allowed CBW-LA to move from Meetup group to registered 501(c)3 non-profit and take one more step toward educating writers throughout the Los Angeles region on their path to writing success.

To all of our former board members—Lena Chen, Amanda Touchton, Jennifer Bailey and Nandini Dev—thank you for your equity in time and talent. We are grateful for the indelible mark that you left on our group.

To all of our current board members—Lucy Ravitch, Tiffani Barth, Angie Flores and Alana Garrigues—thank you for your love, support and ideas.

To the Caravan Rug Corporation, thank you for sharing your office supplies and allowing CBW-LA to use the printer, paper and ink necessary to conduct workshops.

To Albertson's, Trader Joe's, and Panera, thank you for feeding us during such a long day of creative thought.

To the Torrance Municipal Airport, thank you for allowing us to host our Anthology Launch party in such a beautiful location.

To all of our speakers in 2013—Arlee Bird, Cassandra Black, Samantha Combs, Reece Michaelson, Carmen Rodrigues and Pamela Jay Smith—thank you, from the bottom of our hearts, for the inspiration, insight and courage you bring to our members. We are all better, more thoughtful authors thanks to your advice.

To Nutschell Anne Windsor, your vision and your friendship have made us stronger in talent and community than any of us could have imagined. Thank you.

www.ingramcontent.com/pod-product-compliance
Lightning Source LLC
Chambersburg PA
CBHW060316260626
47160CB00007B/2638